COLIN HUNTER

TWO WHEELS

AND A WILL

The motivational story of ultra-cyclists exploring their limits on the ultimate bikepacking adventure

Copyright 2021 © Jean-Philippe Soulé (writing as Colin Hunter)

All rights reserved. No part of this publication may be reproduced, stored or transmitted in any form or by any means, electronic, mechanical, photocopying, recording, scanning, or otherwise without written permission from the publisher. It is illegal to copy this book, post it to a website, or distribute it by any other means without permission.

First Edition

ISBN: 979-8-9852426-1-4 Paperback
ISBN: 978-0-9843448-8-8 e-Book

Published by Native Planet Adventures
www.jeanphilippesoule.com

Notes

I hope this book will not only be of interest to endurance athletes but also be enjoyed by anyone interested in sports, travel, adventure, or how and why people explore their physical and mental limits. It isn't a training guidebook or an instruction manual on how to start bikepacking, but I included a few sections that explain basic information about power, nutrition, and training zones that may interest those who are getting into the sport. I've tried to explain these fundamentals as simply as possible. For each optional section, a subject icon will mark the title.

🏔 This mountain icon defines an optional technical section that should be of particular interest to cyclists or endurance athletes.

🏰 This castle icon indicates an optional section with cultural or historical insights.

You can skip an optional section and jump right back into the race. The story will flow smoothly whether you read these optional insights or choose to skip them.

French accent marks

This book takes place in the Pyrenees. Since I am writing in English, throughout the book Pyrenees will have no French accent marks when used as an English name. Pyrénées will be spelled in French with the acute accents (é) when it's part of one of the specific French regions. France is divided into geopolitical regions. The Pyrenees mountain chain is made of five regions. From west to east these are *Pyrénées-Atlantiques* (which includes the two ethnic regions of *Pays-Basque* and *Béarn*), *Hautes-Pyrénées*, *Haute-Garonne*, *Ariège,* and *Pyrénées-Orientales*. When addressing these specific regions, I will use the French spelling for Pyrénées, with the acute accents. But I will often refer to the Oriental Pyrenees with the English spelling to describe all the Pyrenees mountains east of the central *Hautes-Pyrénées* region. Thus, for example, mentioning a climb such as *Port de Pailhères* as being an Oriental Pyrenees climb, even though it is located in the region of *Ariège*, and not within the geopolitical border of the *Pyrénées-Orientales*.

Distances and weight

Weights are expressed in kilograms and often abbreviated as kg.
1 kg = 2.2 lbs.
Distances are expressed in kilometers and often abbreviated as km.
1 km = 0.62 mi.
Speed is expressed in kilometer per hour and is abbreviated as km/h.

Contents

Introduction	1
Lining up for the Tourmalet Pursuit	15
The Road to Mur de Péguère	23
On the Way to the Mediterranean Sea	63
Pailhères, the Oriental Giant	77
Welcome Back to the Hautes-Pyrénées	95
Tourmalet for Dessert	103
On to the Hautacam Pursuit	115
Day Six of the Ultimate Pyrenees & Day One of the Hautacam Pursuit	125
Race to the Atlantic	139
Flying over Mountains	149
All Kinds of Pain	157
Alone and Still Going	165
It Doesn't Get Any Better	169

In Pursuit of Life-Changing Challenges	183
Racing across Europe	189
More Books by the Author	193

Introduction

A New Ultra-Endurance Experience

The Tour de France, known as the world's toughest race, is beyond grueling: 21 days during which the world's best professional endurance athletes battle it on endless mountain roads. It's so epic that millions of fans from all over the world come to witness it live and cheer the living legends that push their bodies to unimaginable pain levels.

Imagine a cycling event covering a similar distance with three times the elevation gain and half the time to accomplish it, with a fully loaded bike.

Self-sufficiency and a never-stopping clock… No massage. No salary. No prize money. No podium… Just sheer mountain beauty and pain.

An elevation gain of 66,000 meters over 2700 kilometers crossing rugged mountains makes the Ultra Bike Pursuit unlike any other road cycling race in the world. It's like climbing Everest 20 times from its base camp in less than 12 days.

Is that even possible? Could anybody achieve such a thing? Would anybody even attempt it?

Following five ultra-cyclists racing across the Pyrenees mountains as they push beyond their physical limits, I will try to show how people can achieve the seemingly unachievable, and what inspires ultra-endurance athletes to put their bodies through intense levels of pain. You will discover breathtaking mountain landscapes, gasp for air as you experience the hardship of this sport, but you will also witness their greatest moments and understand what drives them.

Ultra-endurance

What is ultra-endurance, and ultra-cycling?

Endurance athletes push their limits. Ultra-endurance athletes go beyond. Ultra-endurance is the ultimate pursuit of pushing your body beyond its physical limits, which I'll sometimes refer to as exploring your limits.

For the uninitiated, it may seem like a meaningless masochist quest, a futile pursuit of pain.

Why push yourself beyond anything humanly possible? Why go through so much suffering?

If it were only about pain, ultra-endurance sports wouldn't be some of the fastest-growing sport trends.

These athletes achieve what they do simply because they refuse to accept the words *unachievable* or *impossible*. The body has its limits; the mind doesn't. To quote my youth motto as narrated in my memoir *I, Tarzan: Against All Odds*, "It's all in the head." And it's only once we explore our physical and mental limits that we discover who we really are. It's a transformative life experience—but is it for everybody?

Are ultra-endurance athletes superhuman? Do ultra-cyclists all have a 32-bpm resting heart rate, a 92 VO2 Max, and a lean, perfectly sculpted muscular body?

They certainly don't all have freaky natural abilities, but yes, they are superhumans. Not for their strength, and not for their look. You could never tell an ultra-endurance cyclist from an everyday recreational one only from his or her look. They are often physically gifted with extreme endurance abilities, the fruit of years of outdoor sports, but that's not what makes an ultra-endurance athlete. So what sets them apart?

I will try to unveil exactly this by following these ultra-cyclists on their 2020 attempt at riding through the pristine mountains of the French Pyrenees in a new road cycling event like no other. I invite you to meet these extraordinary people—ultra-cyclists on a quest for enlightenment. As they take on one of the most incredible challenges, they will inspire you to go further, make you believe in your own dreams, and help you reach the goals you always thought to be impossible.

And even though it takes special people to attempt such an adventure, will any of them be able to cross that impossible finish line in only 12 days, and rise to become a bikepacking legend?

Before we dive into their ultra-endurance world, let me introduce myself.

The organizer

My name is Jean-Philippe Soulé[1]. I am French (although I also have a US passport). I have lived on four continents and traveled to over 64 countries, becoming fluent in five languages. I have spent my entire life as an explorer-adventurer in the most remote regions of the planet, leading mountain, jungle, and ocean expeditions, from speed-mountaineering in France and trekking high-altitude Himalayan mountains in my youth, to running the length of the Pyrenees before the sport of trail running even existed, to months spent trekking and living in the densest tropical jungle, to a three-year, death-defying, 5000-kilometre sea-kayaking adventure[2] across Central America on the wild Pacific and Atlantic oceans, to ultra-cycling in my 50s. Ultra-endurance has guided and molded my being.

In 2002, I was a guide and USA Cycling coach in Seattle, the head of a cycling club, organizer of long-distance road bike mountain climbing fundraising events, and a track racer. In 2007, I moved back to my native Pyrenees. I combined my experience of the outdoors, endurance sports,

---
1. I am an award-winning and bestselling author of real-life adventure and travel memoirs published under my full name, Jean-Philippe Soulé. I also write in other genres, using pen names to differentiate among them. Colin Hunter is my pseudonym for cycling books.
2. Documented in my first book, *Dancing with Death*.

leading expeditions, cycling, and my intimate knowledge of the Pyrenees regions to design and guide unique cycling tours[3] for mountain lovers of all abilities.

My quest has always been to use sports to experience fabulous landscapes and immerse myself in the most fascinating cultures. I designed cycling tours with these components as the backbone to offer cyclists the experience of a lifetime, all while enjoying the greatest level of comfort, and the best of local food and services. I spent the full decade of my 40s guiding cyclists on the mountain roads of the Tour de France, Vuelta a España, and Giro d'Italia.

My days of racing my bike on a track were years behind me. I was no longer tasting the blood in my throat, or coughing, gasping for air after an intense pursuit session riding at the maximum heart rate I could possibly sustain. I returned to my root of climbing mountains and endurance quests. When time would allow, as it often conflicted with my guiding season, I entered mountain *cyclosportives*[4].

In 2016, to celebrate my 50th birthday, I decided to cross the Pyrenees on a mountain itinerary that I had guided numerous times over the previous 12 years. It's generally done in seven full and challenging days, but to remove that oppressive feeling of the weight of a half-century suddenly upon me, I wanted to ride it in three. It was also a nod at the Pyrenees crossing I had done running when I was 20 years old: proof to myself that, even 30 years later and without any specific training, I was still alive with many more years of endurance sport and adventures ahead of me. It was my first taste of ultra-endurance on a bike and a successful experience I longed to repeat.

I also completed the longest one-day ultra-cycling events in the mountains with the 320-kilometer, 6000-meter Luchon-Bayonne that same year, followed in July 2017 by the 330-kilometer, 8000-meter Tour du Mont-

---

3. See www.velotopo.com
4. A "cyclosportive" is an organized, mass participation cycling event where participants can challenge themselves against the clock over typically long and arduous courses.

Blanc race. (The second number in meters depicts the elevation gain, which is even more significant than the distance for mountain challenges.)

My wife, Yumi, an accomplished mountain endurance road cyclist, had placed first and fourth woman respectively in the Luchon-Bayonne and Tour du Mont-Blanc mountain races. Tour du Mont-Blanc was the holy grail of one-day mountain road cycling events. She wanted something tougher to test her limits, but it seemed nothing could challenge her more than that event.

So in March 2019, she searched the internet for her ultimate summer challenge. One day she told me she had found a 7400-kilometer non-stop race across Europe from Norway to Spain that crossed the Alps and 15 countries. Less than a dozen solo cyclists had crossed the finish line the previous year, and no pair succeeded. She wanted us to enter as a pair and set the record. We would be the first.

This is how, at the age of 53, I discovered the sport of ultra-bikepacking—and what an experience it was. It was a revelation. But that will be the subject of my next cycling book[5]. Racing across Europe was my inspiration to design a spectacular and unique ultra-bikepacking event: the subject of this story.

Bikepacking

Bikepacking is still a young sport and remains fairly unknown to the global cycling community. When you're backpacking on a bike, you are bikepacking.

Bike touring is more than a century old, but bikepacking was born when cyclists moved away from the huge bags that were set on rear and front racks, to only use small, soft, ultra-light bags. They switched from carrying all the gear for comfort and all contingencies to the bare minimum in order to travel light and fast. For long bikepacking events, people may take a 15-liter saddle bag, a seven-liter frame bag, and a five-liter handlebar

---

5. Read the Addendum about racing across Europe.

bag, while traditional touring bikes were often loaded with a minimum of 100 or more liters of gear.

On ultra-bikepacking events, racers often only take one or two much smaller bags. Some even only use a single seven-liter bag and nothing else. This follows a trend that happened in mountain climbing in the 1980s, when solo mountaineers started speed climbing, leaving behind all the traditional expedition equipment. It later happened in trekking with people replacing heavy loaded backpacks with ultralight water carrying vests and not much more, a trend that gave birth to the sport of ultra-trail running. This decade is the bikepacking revolution with new events mushrooming around the world.

In an ultra-bikepacking event, from the start you carry with you any pieces of equipment, clothing, or supplies you think you may need. There are no organized feed stations. There is no assistance team. No private resupply. No private lodging. Support vehicles aren't allowed.

You can purchase anything you want during the event. Services you use must always be commercially available to all participants and not pre-arranged. You may eat at restaurants or cafes, or buy food in any commercial venue. You can choose to sleep on the side of the road with a mere survival blanket, a bivvy bag (a waterproof, thin shell layer like a sleeping bag), or a tent, or you can stay in hotels and other commercial accommodation along the way.

The word *ultra-bikepacking*, already in use for a few years, has not yet been formally defined. I don't think it can be done using standard measures, not by distance, not by elevation, because cyclists of all abilities will experience it differently. If you go on a long bike holiday, using cycling more as a means of transport than a sport, you are bikepacking. Even if you ride around the world, it's not automatically considered ultra. I think that whether you climb seven mountains or none, over a daily distance that could range from a mere 100 to over 400 kilometers, if you're pushing yourself more than eight hours a day two days in a row at a sustained pace, you are ultra-bikepacking. There is no clear line between ultra- and bikepacking when you bike travel on your own. You define your sport based on the intensity at which you ride. When you enter an event longer than 24 hours either timed or with a time limit, you are ultra-bikepacking. In this book, I will use both the words *bikepacking* and *bikepacker* without always repeating the word *ultra*, to refer to the extreme endurance sport of ultra-bikepacking.

Apart from fighting gravity in the mountains, overcoming wind resistance is the greatest effort required of a cyclist. When riding a few centimeters behind another cyclist, you cut a significant amount of the wind resistance. It's called drafting. When riding inside a *peloton* (bunch) of cyclists, shielded by others, that wind resistance becomes negligible. This is why pro cyclists are able to race at averages of 50 km/h, because only those taking turns at the front produce the effort necessary to fight the incredible wind resistance generated by high speeds. The team leaders usually rest comfortably in the middle of the peloton, saving most of their energy for the mountains or final sprint. Ultra-cyclists don't have the drafting advantage of a large bunch. Nobody helps you save energy, and you must earn each kilometer forward.

The greatest challenge is that the clock never stops. Once you launch from the start line, the event will only stop after you cross the finish.

Some cyclists, whose main goal is to cross the finish within the event time limit, may sleep full nights to be well rested for the daily challenges. Those aiming to be at the front will have little sleep, if any at all. Riding at night is part of the adventure and a new experience for many.

This is not a professional race. Most professional wouldn't accept to endure this.

Pro cyclists race in a peloton four to six hours a day before they receive a massage, enjoy expertly prepared meals, and rest in a comfortable bed. Ultra-bikepackers rarely stop, some rarely sleep. They eat what they carry or find on the way. When an ultra-cyclist climbs a mountain, it's with a bike loaded with bags and gear. His or her effort is exponentially harder than those of a pro racer.

Bikepackers are a new breed of ultra-cyclists looking to explore their physical and mental limits and push beyond. Bikepacking is cycling in its purest form. Like an artist, you craft your life with each pedal stroke. Ultra-cycling is your masterpiece. It combines the sport of cycling with extreme endurance, travel, and adventure: many of the things that have driven my life. It's the essence of freedom.

Bikepacking events are in some ways similar to the Tour de France races in the early 20th century, when cyclists received no assistance, carried their spare tires around their shoulders, and covered incredible distances. But even then, they still raced in stages with enough sleeping time to partly recover. Bikepacking events have only one single stage, a never-ending multi-day-and-night stage. There is no planned rest. When the day ends, the clock keeps rolling, and so do the cyclists.

The sport may also take its sources from the early Paris-Brest-Paris events, first promoted in 1891 in the *Petit Journal* as an event where self-sufficient riders carrying their own food and clothing would race the 1200 kilometers from Paris to Brest and back. Though pro cyclists abandoned the Paris-Brest-Paris to move on to race the Tour de France, decades later amateurs called *randonneurs* gave it a second life. Today the PBP, as it's known, draws thousands of participants and has given birth to numerous similar or shorter events around the world.

Although these events were already ultra-endurance adventures, the 2013 inaugural 3000-kilometer Transcontinental Race (TCR) brought a new dimension to the meaning of ultra-cycling. In 2014, the 4200-mile (6800-km) Trans Am Bike Race (TABR), crossing the entire United States from Pacific to Atlantic, claimed the title of world's longest road cycling race. These races have gained huge popularity and many similar races on roads, gravel, and trails have since mushroomed all around the world.

The TABR remained the world's longest road race until the 2018 inauguration of the NorthCape-Tarifa (NCT), covering 7400 kilometers from Norway to Spain. The itinerary, crossing parts of the Alps and other mountains in France and Spain, was also advertised as the world's toughest. It's a claim many other organizers like to label their events with. When so many extreme endurance cycling events are offered in different terrains and climates, it's hard to compare and judge which takes the lead. Some of these races are done on road bikes, others on mountain bikes, and more and more now on gravel bikes. But until 2019, the NCT was not only the longest, but maybe also the world's toughest road cycling event.

Birth of the Ultra Bike Pursuit

My wife and I raced the NCT 2019 edition to become the first pair to ever cross the finish line in Tarifa. Crossing 15 countries, riding around the clock was a grand experience that inspired me.

Claims of being the world's longest or toughest aren't what's important in these extreme ultra-endurance races. The experience is what matters most. And that is dictated by various factors, which will differ for all cyclists. As a long-time ultra-endurance athlete and world explorer, I have spent my entire life seeking extreme challenges but always combined with equally extreme discoveries. It is an ongoing quest to immerse myself in the most beautiful scenery or unique cultural experience. The sport alone does not fulfill me as much as what it allows me to explore and find beyond the physical activity. Combined with amazing landscapes, it reaches a new dimension.

Cycling is an endurance sport that gives you a tremendous feeling of freedom while allowing you to discover some of the world's fascinating landscapes. Bikepacking pushes this even further. You're no longer limited. You could cross a mountain range, a country, a continent, or more. Suddenly, the entire world is yours, and you could start pedaling from your home to discover it.

As much as I loved the experience of crossing Europe on a bicycle, and recommend it, there were some long dull sections, and roads with too much heavy and fast motorized traffic to my taste; roads on which I would normally never choose to ride. Not all European countries are well suited to road cycling. I loved the experience, but on sections where I either felt for our safety, or just couldn't see the landscape change for hours, I kept dreaming of a multi-day event where every single kilometer would offer constant change with some of the best mountain scenery unfolding before your eyes, on quiet roads where you wouldn't be stressed by fast cars and trucks.

I knew that over a shorter distance, the Pyrenees alone would offer as much challenge, with more spectacular scenery than even the world's longest race across 15 countries. What sets the Pyrenees apart is the combination of the most legendary climbs of the Tour de France, with a network of quiet and scenic mountain roads. I've guided cyclists on the overcrowded Alpe-d'Huez and Stelvio climbs upon request but ask me for the most amazing cycling spots and I'll name you dozens of mountains you've never heard of, that are far more beautiful, and even more challenging. In 15 years of organizing and guiding exclusive tours to the best regions of France, Spain, and Italy, I've always preferred these to the more famous ones.

I felt compelled to design an event that encompassed all that I love about cycling and the mountains. I wanted each kilometer to be a stunning revelation. My vision was to ensure every road would be enjoyable to cycle. I wanted to design an ultra-cycling event that represented me as a person, a summary of my life as a mountaineer, a cycling guide, and a world adventurer—fueled by my deep love and extensive knowledge of *my* mountains. An event in continuity with my life pursuit of extreme challenges, extreme beauty, and extreme discovery.

I wanted to share all my passion with my fellow cyclists by designing the ultimate challenge that I dreamed of doing myself, a challenge both awesomely spectacular and so impossibly difficult that even with proper training, I wouldn't be certain to cross the finish line. The Ultra Bike Pursuit.

The drive of doubts and uncertainty

The Pyrenees mountain chain has been the ground of the fiercest cycling battles since the 1910 Tour de France, and some of its climbs such as Tourmalet, Hautacam, Luz-Ardiden, and Aubisque are legendary. They lure amateur cyclists in the thousands, flocking to France each year to ride these iconic mountain climbs emulating their idols. But the Pyrenees are also known for quiet, remote mountain wilderness, and they hide many more secret gems. Climbs that are even more scenic than the legendary ones, and even tougher. The Ultra Bike Pursuit would combine most of the famous Tour de France climbs with many off-the-beaten-path mountains that even some local cyclists have never set wheels on.

An elevation gain of 66,000 meters may mean little to non-cyclists. To put things into perspective, the climb of Mount Everest from its base camp yields a 3250-meter elevation gain, which is why riding the Ultra Bike Pursuit event is like climbing Everest 20 times in a row. Attempting to do it in a maximum of 288 hours or 12 days is madness. Cyclists, at least any normal human beings, can't do that. But as the organizer and designer of the Ultra Bike Pursuit, I wanted it to be the epitome of spectacular mountain beauty and a challenge to even the world's best ultra-cyclists.

I intimately knew every climb and every road of my native Pyrenees, and I wasn't even certain that I'd be able to ride this entire itinerary within 288 hours. I wondered how many cyclists could.

For 50 years, I've imagined challenges and expeditions that seemed unachievable. My family and friends questioned my sanity, asking me why I would ever want to attempt something impossible. Why suffer or risk your life to attempt something when your chance of success is close to zero? It was a recurring question for decades. My entire life, I envisioned impossible challenges for myself. And now, for the first time, I was doing it for others.

When I first talked about the Ultra Bike Pursuit concept to my friends, their feedback echoed what I had heard for years. This time they asked: "Why design an event that most people couldn't complete?"

It is not crossing a finish line that motivates me. It is the doubts and uncertainty of being able to accomplish something that makes it exponentially more interesting. It is in front of the greatest challenge and adversity that you find your true self. And this is with this philosophy that I imagined and designed this event.

Introduction

After months of carefully crafting and re-crafting every part of the route, I was pleased with the itinerary. I had designed the most spectacular and toughest ultra-cycling event I could think of. But I also quickly realized that it was too hard. I knew the difficulty level would turn away the large majority of ultra-cyclists.

All want the bragging rights and the coveted T-shirt that says "Finisher"—not for the T-shirt itself, of course, but for what it represents, success after an incredible effort. But many cyclists prefer flatter courses and to tackle a challenge when they are almost certain they will be able to cross the finish line.

Only a rare breed of free-minded adventure spirits would consider this ultimate mountain cycling event. And they also would need to be accomplished endurance cyclists. That further narrowed the potential number of participants.

When I started talking about it with my ultra-cycling friends, all said:

"*That's crazy!*"

"*¡Esto es Loco!*"

"*L'Ultra, Oui, mais ça, c'est barjo!*"

"*Questo è pazzesco!*"

"*It's too difficult. Sorry, but not for me.*"

I was talking to people who had raced across America and Europe. I was talking to famous ultra-endurance cyclists who had numerous podiums on their records. I was talking to the bikepacking and adventure bike racing stars. Most preferred a course with less elevation. Many told me they thought it was too difficult.

I had spent days and nights for over half a year designing the ultimate cycling adventure challenge to realize that finding even a half-dozen participants proved impossible.

I understood that to get anybody to line up at the start, I also had to offer other, shorter routes.

When designing shorter alternatives, I didn't want to compromise by removing any of the spectacular scenery. I kept the original itinerary untouched. I called it the Ultimate Pyrenees Pursuit. And I divided it into two halves, an eastern and a western part that I respectively named the Tourmalet and Hautacam Pursuits[6], bearing the names of their last mountain climbs.

These were still too hard to attract a large number of cyclists, so from these two halves, I stripped some climbs and offered a shorter option for each of the Tourmalet and Hautacam Pursuits. For each Pursuit, cyclists had a choice of a 500-km Discovery course, or the original Hardcore route. The Discovery courses preserved the essence of both the Tourmalet and Hautacam Pursuits, but broke them into events all bikepackers and even cyclists new to ultras and bikepacking could venture into. The 500 km with a five-day limit allowed for a daily average of 100 km, something most cyclists could attain. The Hardcore routes each packed more climbs and elevation gain per kilometer, enough to challenge the most experienced ultra-cyclists.

That made a total of four optional routes in addition to the original 2700-km Ultimate Pyrenees Pursuit.

The 2020 event

It was originally designed to feature over 50 major mountain climbs, more than in any other events. A couple of weeks before the start, with a growing COVID risk in Spain and Andorra, I slightly trimmed the itinerary to keep the entire event within the boundaries of France, reducing the Ultimate Pyrenees to 43 major climbs over 2300 km with 55,000 m gain. It still meant a huge elevation gain equivalent to 17 ascents of Everest. The Tourmalet Pursuit would be 1100 km and the Hautacam Pursuit 1200 km. The Discovery loops remained unchanged.

It's never easy to launch a new event, particularly one perceived by many to be too difficult. COVID further limited the field of participants. A few people canceled a few days prior to departure due to possible quarantine restrictions imposed by their country of residence. Many others who

---

6. In 2021, I renamed these the Catalan and Basque Pursuits.

Introduction

also wanted to attempt one of the Ultra Bike Pursuit courses could not travel from the USA, Canada, Australia, Brazil, or even from countries as close as the UK.

The French Pyrenees, with a very low population density and no major cities, was one of the least affected regions of France and the risk was low. Despite COVID preventing most people from traveling, I was determined not to cancel the event, even though it meant running it at a loss. It wasn't a commercial bet from the beginning, but more of a dream of producing an event that allowed me to share with others my passion for the sport with the love of my native Pyrenees mountains. Passion had always been the driving factor in my life, and COVID wouldn't change that.

And so it was with a small group of five participants spread over four different courses that the Ultra Bike Pursuit started on September 6. Two would be taking on the Tourmalet Pursuit. Two more people would start the Hautacam Pursuit five days later. And one young man, Pierre Charles, joined the two first cyclists at the start of the Tourmalet Pursuit but would continue to ride the Hautacam Pursuit without any break, thus attempting to be the very first to finish the full Ultimate Pyrenees Pursuit.

These five ultra-cyclists would push their limits beyond their wildest imagination. Regardless of whether they crossed the finish line or not, all five participants' journeys, experiences, and achievements will inspire you. This is their story.

Chapter 1

Lining up for the Tourmalet Pursuit

The Tourmalet Pursuit[1] would take cyclists over a succession of mountain passes and through deep gorges from the mountain town of Bagnères-de-Bigorre in the heart of the French Pyrenees all the way to the Mediterranean Sea – and back. The route covered 1100 km with 22,000 m of climbing.

I would drive the entire course around the clock, sometimes even sleeping a few hours on the side of the road, to meet with them as often as possible. This would allow me to be present at some of the checkpoints, but also to interact with them and check on their physical and mental states, encourage them, and document all the details of some of their greatest and most painful moments.

I first met with the three participants on the afternoon of September 5, the eve of the event. There, after welcoming them, I described the route, reminded them of the event rules, explained the use of the satellite tracker and briefed them on safety. I then checked their bikes and mandatory equipment and gave them their bib numbers they fixed on their bikes. It was also the first time they all met. They were relaxed and exchanged stories about their experience or lack thereof.

The three people lining up on the start line could not have been more different, and so were their experiences in ultra-cycling and level of train-

---
1. Renamed the Catalan Pursuit from 2021.

ing. But even more different were their goals. Bikepacking is unlike any other type of bike race or event. You don't participate to race against others. You compete with others against yourself. Other participants are a source of inspiration. Each has their own goals. And crossing the finish line is only one of them. It's not the destination, but the journey that matters most in ultra bikepacking. And the journey of a lifetime lay ahead of them.

Blond, fair skin, blue eyes, Pierre Charles with his muscular thighs didn't look as skinny as he was. For his 1m79, he only weighed a featherlight 54 kg. At age 28, he was the youngest but most experienced and trained ultra-distance cyclist of the three. He works as a bike messenger hauling big weights, riding a laden cargo bike around the hills of the city of Lyon. He'd been racing ultra-bikepacking events for a few years and placed eighth and third in a race across France that included a crossing of the Alps.

Pierre does not use a car, and hardly ever any public transportation. Everywhere he goes is by bicycle. In 2019, he had ridden more kilometers than many pro cyclists. For 2020, he had a goal of accumulating an even greater mileage than the previous year, even though he was confined like everybody else in France with a national government law that forbade outside cycling for two months during that first wave of COVID.

Pierre loves nothing more than climbing mountains, and he had never cycled the Pyrenees. When he stumbled upon the event, the promised itinerary captivated him so much he signed up instantly. He said the longest Ultra Bike Pursuit looked like his dream event. Then he spotted the line on the website about the Ultimate Pyrenees Pursuit that read:

We challenge you to complete the longest Hardcore loops of both challenges back-to-back in less than 12 days (a feat we don't expect anyone to accomplish on their first attempt).

I wrote this last statement as a hook to arouse curiosity and challenge ultra-cyclists, and it worked. That immediately became his goal. He would be among the very first to attempt it. He would start riding the Tourmalet Pursuit with Chris and Yvonnick, then continue with the Hautacam Pursuit that Alex and Guillaume were scheduled to start on September 11.

Where would Pierre be by that time? Would he be ahead of them? A day behind? Or would he even still be in the game to attempt the second part? The six-day deadline of the first eastern route does not only apply to participants of the Tourmalet Pursuit event. Pierre also needed to complete that first part within the same deadline to be allowed to continue onto the western route.

Chris Jackson is an experienced ultra-bikepacker from the UK. Having just celebrated his 61st birthday, he was the oldest participant in this year's event, proving that age isn't a limiting factor to practice and perform in ultra-cycling.

He had previously been a sponsored windsurfer and didn't have much cycling experience before 2016, but he hired a coach seven months prior to his first ultra-bikepacking race in 2017 and caught the ultra-bikepacking bug. Over a three-year period, his cycling coach helped him increase his power to a phenomenal 296 watts[2]. But he would later say that his absolute best training was the Ultra Bike Pursuit itself, which after some rest, brought his power up to 319 watts.

Chris was very well organized, both with his gear and his meticulous planning. He told me that he had researched every place on the itinerary and planned all food stops, marking them in his GPS. Standing at 1m88, Chris was not only tall, lean, and physically tough, he seemed to have clear intent. From the start, he said, *"No hotel stays for me. I'll sleep in the rain if I have to."* He then said *"Check into a hotel and you check out of the adventure. I'm in it for the adventure not the hotels."*

It had been a long training and time commitment, and for three years he had not focused on work or social life. Many of his 2019 ultra-cycling projects had failed for various reasons. He was registered for a couple of events in 2020 for which he'd trained hard, and those were canceled because of the COVID. It was a long series of disappointments, and he was losing motivation. He had started to doubt whether ultra-cycling really was

---

2. Power is the combination of force we apply on the pedals multiplied by velocity, which is the number of pedal rotations per minute. The result is expressed in watts. Not many recreational cyclists can sustain a 300-watt power for an hour. The section "Weight, Power & FTP" in Chapter 2 will provide more in depth information.

worth his time commitment, but he was inspired to explore his limits with the thrill, camaraderie and challenge of an organized event.

That's when he found the Ultra Bike Pursuit. The 1100-km Tourmalet Pursuit Hardcore loop was perfect for him: an incredible challenge he could fit into his schedule. And living in France, he wasn't affected by the quarantine restrictions his native UK had imposed on all travelers returning home. He was already trained, having prepared for the other events. He also had all the gear necessary and with three years of bikepacking experience, he felt ready.

That morning, just before the start, Chris made a hotel reservation for September 9 for his return to the finish in Bagnères-de-Bigorre. He was hoping to cross the finish line in less than four days.

I had no doubt that Chris was a strong and experienced ultra-cyclist, but surely he underestimated the challenge of the never-ending Pyrenees climbs? Finishing the Tourmalet Pursuit in less than six days would be an accomplishment. Four days would require superhuman powers. There is a big danger in underestimating a challenge. Would Chris make the mistake of riding too fast and sleeping too little to chase after an impossible time?

And there was Yvonnick Brossier, gray-haired, 1m71, and slim, a 54-year-old medical doctor who co-owned and managed his own clinic in the Pyrenees. Yvonnick had never ridden any multi-day bikepacking events, but he had lived and trained in the Pyrenees for twenty years, regularly training on all the Hautes-Pyrénées mountain passes. Still, it would be his first time on many of the climbs and rural roads of the Eastern Pyrenees.

In addition to his medical practice, the management of the clinic did not allow him much training time. Yvonnick signed up having done less than 4600 kilometers over the first six months of the year, and only had three months to train for what was by far the longest, toughest ride he'd ever done. Because he can only train on weekends, he commutes on his bike 10 kilometers to work each way, year around, regardless of the weather; even on the cold winter days, as long as the road isn't icy. Nevertheless, a 10-kilometer commute can hardly be training for an ultra-cycling event.

But it was not the long-distance cycling and multiple mountain climbs he was most worried about. He wasn't confident about navigation. He had never followed a course with a GPS. He didn't even own one and had purchased his first real GPS for this event.

He knew nothing about equipment and his night cycling experience was limited to his 10-kilometer morning and evening commutes to work in the winter. But Yvonnick was a good climber who loved mountains much more than the flatter roads of the lower valleys. And he had also done a couple of long-distance rides through France on his own.

He and I were both members of the same local cycling club, and being the same age, he had followed online with great interest when I entered the bikepacking race across Europe the previous year. Later, that February, I had invited Yvonnick to join me in a Bikingman race in the Sultana of Oman. He could not join but was inspired as he followed me once more with the live tracking. He really wanted to try bikepacking.

When I told Yvonnick I was organizing an ultra-cycling event in the Pyrenees, he immediately registered. It was for him the best opportunity to try out this new sport. He could test himself on the mountain terrain he was particularly fond of, in a region he knew, without having to travel far. He lived 20 kilometers from the start and the finish. He couldn't have hoped for an event closer to home. The itinerary even passed less than two kilometers from his house.

He felt confident three months were enough for him to reach a fitness level that would allow him to complete the full Tourmalet Pursuit Hardcore course. But could he really do it, with so little time to train? Being a good climber on a short day with one or two mountain passes was quite different from what Yvonnick had registered for. And with no experience in multi-day ultra-bikepacking, no navigation experience, and few kilometers in his legs, would Yvonnick be ready and able even to complete the 1100-km Hardcore Tourmalet Pursuit within the six-day deadline?

Chapter 1

Most people would have started with the 500-km Discovery Pursuit that was designed to be the perfect introduction to the sport. But not Yvonnick. Go big or stay home was his motto. And confidence and mental strength are often more important than physical training. He had that.

The next few days would reveal what these three gentlemen were made of and whether they underestimated the event they had registered for or overestimated their abilities. Whether they'd live their dreams, or see them shattered with pain and disappointment. Anything could happen in such a challenging event, and not even the best physical and mental preparation could be enough to guarantee success. The journey, though, promised to be epic.

And what better way to follow this grand adventure than being a dot-watcher?

A spectator sport

What is dot-watching?

Everybody knows the Tour de France. Along with the soccer World Cup and Formula 1 Grand Prix, it's one of the most widely broadcasted sport events on the planet. You can turn on your TV from anywhere in the world and not miss any of the action. Cycling fans also enjoy watching the other Grand Tours and classic races. But there isn't any coverage of non-professional races.

Or at least, there wasn't until recently. Now a new trend in ultra-endurance racing allows you to follow the races live via satellite on an online map, watching the moving dots that represent each participant. It's actually called dot-watching, and the fans who follow racers online are dot-watchers. Cyclists all carry a satellite tracker that updates their position every five minutes so you can watch their progression either on a regular map, or even on Google Earth with 3D representations of the mountains they are climbing.

With the Ultra Bike Pursuit, we made dot-watching of your friends and all the other cyclists even more fun. On the website, we posted detailed graphics of each climb profile. You could view the average gradient for each kilometer for every climb. When you saw them approaching a mountain on the live map, you could view all the detailed information about it and get a sense of the challenge they were facing. You could see what were the steepest percentages and where they were located on the climb. You could further view all the mountain relief of where they were on Google Earth, read the informative blurb about it, and see some photos. Even the Tour de France does not always provide this information. And every day, we posted updates on the blog and photos on Instagram. So, it was exciting to dot-watch and follow the Ultra Bike Pursuit.

As the organizer, dot-watching also allowed me to locate all participants, know what climb they were on, at what speed they were riding, how long they stopped, and where would be the best spot for me to go meet them next.

You don't have to know a participant, or even be a cyclist to enjoy dot-watching. Many dot-watchers will follow every race they find and will tell you that following racers live on maps[3] is at least as much fun as watching a stage of the Tour de France.

---

3. You can visit www.ultrabikepursuit.com and replay the 2020 full event, controlling the replay speed from a two-minute speedy résumé to the actual riding pace if you wish to relive every moment. It's a lot of fun that will allow you to experience the entire story you're reading about in this book. But it's best if you try it after finishing the book to avoid any spoilers, because the suspense starts now.

Chapter 2

The Road to Mur de Péguère (September 6)

We set the start and finish line in the private courtyard of the Carré Py' hotel in the town of Bagnères. This place is often referred to as the old Fignon center, being where the late Laurent Fignon, one of France's greatest champions, had a cycling training center. It is also this same courtyard where the Tour de France cycling statue, which everyone photographs on top of Col du Tourmalet, is kept in the winter. The hotel is located in the southern outskirts of Bagnères at the base of the three mountain passes of Tourmalet, Aspin, and Hourquette d'Ancizan. The wide-open courtyard generally offers views of the mountains to the south, a view denied by this morning's thick cloud layer. The air was unusually fresh and humid for the month of September.

The starts of big events always fill me with a mixture of emotions: anticipation, excitement and fear. Whatever the leading emotion, it's always with a body drenched with adrenaline that I line myself up, and this morning was no different for me, except that I wasn't even riding. I think I was more excited and worried than any of the three participants.

Pierre and Chris looked placid, patiently waiting on the start line with COVID facial-protection masks on. You could sense they had been ready for a long time, maybe days, even weeks or longer. Both came from different regions and had stayed the night in the town of Bagnères. Yvonnick had driven from home and was still trying to adjust things on his bike, looking at and adjusting his clothing and computer at the 08:00 scheduled departure time. Chris and Pierre agreed to wait until he was ready so they could all start together.

It's thus at 08:05, under a drizzle, that participants set their wheels in motion. Although these conditions are usually perfect on shorter one-day events, as it's neither too cold nor too hot, being wet from the start on a multi-day non-stop event can bring other types of challenges.

It was less than a kilometer from the start that the trio started their first climb. The small Col des Palomières marked the entrance to a remote set of valleys with a maze-like network of rural roads that never see any motorized vehicles other than those of the few locals.

The Baronnies as it's called is an area of hills separating isolated villages and farms in valleys so isolated it feels like riding back in time a century or two. I live on the north side of the Baronnies and it's my favorite training ground to ride in the spring and fall when the higher mountain passes are too cold and covered with snow. It's filled with climbs that range between one and four kilometers. Even if some bear the name of col[1], in the scope of this event they are only hills and not counted as any of the official climbs.

A few more hills later, the final one in the Baronnies took participants less than two kilometers from Yvonnick's house. They continued riding on a section of gentle rolling terrain with a view of the superb high-perched cathedral of Saint-Bertrand-de-Comminges. The full itinerary abounds with historical and cultural landmarks.

They quickly made their way to Col des Ares, the first Tour de France mountain climb. Four hours into the ride, Chris was in the lead most of the climb, until Yvonnick passed him 200 meters before the top that they reached at noon. Chris spent less than a minute on top to don a jacket. Yvonnick took a short break to get his on, have a bite to eat, and go to the bathroom, giving a 15-minute lead to Chris.

Pierre was an hour behind. The hotel he stayed at offered a limited breakfast that he supplemented by swallowing a 170-gram tube of sweet concentrated milk just before the start. A children's favorite, it contains

---
1. French for "mountain pass."

55 g of pure sugar per 100 g of sweet milk. For something slightly larger than a toothpaste tube, it packs 500 calories. It can give you a great instant boost of energy, but if you aren't used to this dosage of sugar and to highly concentrated milk, it may be easier to swallow than to digest. Pierre couldn't digest it and, suffering from a stomachache, had to pull over on multiple occasions to relieve himself. Not a great way to start a multi-day cycling challenge. Yvonnick and Chris, meanwhile, were passing each other endlessly. Yvonnick climbed faster, but stopped more often and longer.

Col des Ares with its mild gradient was a gentle climb that wouldn't prepare cyclists for what was to come. It was not even accounted for as one of the official climbs of the event.

Before the cyclists reach the first main climb, let's talk about weight and its crucial importance in an event like this. To illustrate, let's take the examples of Pierre, our lightest cyclist, and of Chris, the heaviest, to which we add the weight of their loaded bikes.

Chris weighs 80 kg and his loaded bike another 15 kg, for a total combined weight of 95 kg.

Pierre weighs 54 kg and his bicycle 11 kg, for a total combined weight of 65 kg.

This combined weight of the cyclist plus his bicycle is what we will now refer to as their weight.

🏔 Weight, Power & FTP

It's a little technical, and without diving into complex scientific or coaching explanations, I will try to keep it as simple as possible so that non-cyclists may understand how weight affects performance in the mountains. If you aren't interested, you may skip this section by clicking on the arrow icon to resume with the epic adventure of our ultra-cyclists.

Chris is able to push a maximum power of 300 watts for one hour. It's something we call FTP (functional threshold power). It's the maximum power output you are able to sustain for a full 60 minutes of effort at your highest intensity. It is not a power output you would ever use on a regular bike ride, for it is not sustainable. A cyclist that would push one hour at that intensity wouldn't be able to ride any longer. The body would need a lot of recovery time before being able to resume cycling optimally. It's so demanding that even to test their FTP, athletes usually ride intensely for a shorter period of time, often 20 or 30 minutes, and use a calculation table to evaluate their FTP, or at what power level they could have ridden if their effort lasted up to a full hour. This power number gives cyclists an excellent measure to calculate training zones (I'll explain training zones later) and for us to understand the importance of weight while climbing.

The final climb of the Tourmalet Pursuit comes after more than 1000 kilometers of intense mountain riding. They will ascend the western slope of Col du Tourmalet. This legendary ascent of the Tour de France is 18.3 km in length and yields 1450 meters of elevation with an average gradient of 7.9%. All our calculations below will be based on this data. A steeper gradient or gentler climb would call for entirely different numbers. But the 7.9% gradient of Tourmalet makes for a good representative number of the Pyrenees climbs and will work perfectly to explain what cyclists are up against when they climb mountains.

Chris has an FTP of 300 watts. This means he's able to push 300 watts of energy through his pedals for a full hour before collapsing. Because 300 watts is a nice round number and easy to work with for the following explanation, let's suppose that Chris could push 300 watts of power not only for an hour, but for the full duration of the Western Tourmalet climb, even if climbing Tourmalet for non-professional cyclists on a loaded bike takes longer than one hour.

If Chris pushed a constant power of 300 watts during his entire Tourmalet climb with a full weight of 95 kg, he would reach the top in 1h26'.

To climb at the same speed and arrive together on top, Pierre with his full weight of 65 kg would only have to push 206 watts.

That's a significant difference in power output necessary to climb at the same speed. It demonstrates the crucial importance of weight.

Let's dive a little deeper into this example.

Cyclists on ultra-endurance rides could never ride their bikes all day long while pushing powers close to their FTP. Let's assume that Chris has fresh legs and can sustain 70% of his FTP. This means that we assume Chris would be able to sustain 210 watts of power for an entire day.

Please note that 70% is an estimate of what an ultra-cyclist may be able to sustain on a one-day event. On multi-day events, the average is more likely to be under 50% of your FTP. But for the sake of this example, let's assume 70%. And that a highly trained ultra-cyclist not suffering from sleep deprivation may be able to sustain 75% or slightly more of his or her FTP. A lesser trained cyclist, or even an experienced one but tired and suffering from sleep deprivation, may have a hard time sustaining 65% of FTP.

For this example, let's keep the 70% sustainable power output and assume that Chris, after riding over 1000 kilometers of mountain roads, will still be able to output 210 watts. Chris would reach the top of Tourmalet in 2h01'. That's a very good time because Chris is a strong cyclist. Not many 80 kg recreational cyclists could manage a 300-watt FTP.

Chris is powerful, but imagine lifting a 30-kg backpack. Some people may not even be able to lift that bag off the ground. Imagine carrying that on your back and getting on your bike. Do you think you could even climb that small hill next to your home? How about climbing an entire mountain range feared by the best professional cyclists in the world? Yet 30 kg is the weight difference between Chris and Pierre.

What power output would Pierre have to sustain to climb at the same speed and reach the top of Tourmalet within the same time?

Only 144 watts!

To climb Tourmalet at the same speed, Chris would have to push a strenuous 210 watts, while Pierre would just need to output 144 watts: that's a substantial difference of energy the two cyclists would expand.

And 144 watts might not be much for Pierre. Pierre does not know his FTP because he doesn't ride with a power meter. Let's assume that as a lighter, but highly trained cyclist, Pierre's FTP is 250 watts. 70% would be 175 watts. 144 watts would only be 58% of his FTP. And Pierre's FTP could be much higher. This means that Pierre could almost effortlessly keep up with Chris, even though Chris is much more powerful (300 watts vs 250 watts FTP). If Pierre would also push at 70% of his FTP, which means the riders would put the same intensity in their effort, he would simply fly by Chris like a rocket and climb much faster without exerting himself any more than Chris.

We've assumed that Chris would be able to still push at 70% of his FTP and output 210 watts on his very last climb. That would be extremely impressive after the itinerary he is about to attempt to ride. Most ultra-cyclists with a 300-watt FTP may be happy to still be pushing 180 watts by the time they reach Tourmalet, and that's if they even succeed in reaching Tourmalet after 1000 kilometers.

⛰ Weight and gravity: Two words that will make you feel a lot of pain

On the eve of the event, you can no longer change your body weight. It's too late to diet and try to shave a kilogram from your belly. But you can still control the weight of your bike and all the gear you are taking. It doesn't matter much on a flat course. It's important on a hilly course, and it's of capital importance on a mountain course such as that of the Ultra Bike Pursuit.

Weight is everything. Each kilogram Chris could shave would save him approximately three watts of effort on every climb; three kilograms make almost a 10-watt difference. It's a huge saving in energy for a cyclist. These numbers work for the average gradient of Tourmalet. The steeper the hill, the more watts saving it would translate into.

Repeated over each mountain each day, the saving wouldn't be in minutes, but in hours. And it's not only about speed and time, after all, not all cyclists entering an ultra-bikepacking event are interested in riding fast. But it's also about the energy you would save to be fresher and have less tired legs day after day.

Even if you could shave a single kilogram off your bike, it makes a world of difference. So, when you think that a piece of equipment is only 200 grams, and another one only weighs 300 grams, you already have two pieces of gear that make a half-kilo. Add a few nuts and energy bars and you're well over a kilo.

Now that you understand the importance of weight while cycling in the mountains, let's talk about packing.

Trimming down

As an ultra-bikepacker, you need to carry all your stuff. You're not allowed to receive outside assistance from family, friends, or a team. You must carry everything you might need with you. That includes clothing, tools, spare parts, drinks, food, pharmacy and toiletry, GPS, phone, satellite tracker, essential lights, and all the batteries or chargers to keep them running.

If you think as an expedition leader, you'll take the best of everything. You'll plan for every contingency so that you can fix any possible problems with your bike, fight the elements no matter how bad the weather you may encounter, get a good night's sleep, take lots of energy drinks, bars, all your favorite food, and of course a toothbrush with toothpaste, soap to smell good all the way, all kinds of cream for your bottom, your muscles, your skin, sunscreen, insect repellents, let's not forget toilet paper, and all the things I'm still forgetting.

You need a trailer to pack your 15 kg of gear, which will be added to your three-kilogram trailer and the weight of your bike. You'll never finish the Ultra Bike Pursuit. You'd quit on the very first climb.

So how do you pack? We've just mentioned that list of all the essential stuff, and we have to remove 90% of it. That's complicated. You need to evaluate what's most important and what trade-off you are willing to make to pack a reasonable amount of gear while keeping your weight to a minimum.

Are you willing to risk having a mechanical problem and being stranded with your bike on the side of the road? This may mean having to scratch[2]. What is the most likely bike maintenance issue you may have? A flat tire? You need a patching kit, spare tubes, a pump (all mandatory items for this event), and maybe even an inflator with CO_2 cartridges. You need some oil for your chain. And maybe a spare derailleur hanger? Breaking it could happen if you drop your bike, whether you crash or just let the wind knock it onto the road from that tree or road sign where you stand it while taking a short break. And none of the local shops will have your specific model. You're out of the race. What else could you need? A spare tire, chain, spokes, brake and gear cables, tools to adjust all parts of your bike that may come loose? You'll need your trailer.

How about clothing? Are you going to assume it won't be cold and only take the mandatory rain jacket, long-finger gloves, night reflective vest, and no change at all? Or do you want to change your bibs once in a while, have a dry under-layer, and warm clothes for the night? Are you afraid of being cold on the descent of a high mountain pass if it's raining and freezing? Are you taking arm and leg warmers, shoe covers, buff neck warmer, a wool hat, a spare pair of thick wool socks and a down jacket? Again, you need a trailer.

How are you going to sleep? The lightest solution is the credit card and stopping in hotels or any other accommodation along the way. That's assuming you find one open where and when you want to stop. But what if you have to spend one night outdoors or plan to sleep out every night? A thin mattress? A light sleeping bag? A waterproof bivvy bag shell? And even maybe an inflating pillow? (I'm joking.)

How about food? Gels, energy bars, dried fruits and nuts, electrolyte powder, some peanut-butter-and-jelly sandwiches? How about first aid? Chamois cream? Sunscreen?

Those are all difficult choices and depend on how much comfort you are willing to sacrifice and the risks you are willing to take. Packing for an ultra-cycling event is an art.

How about you? What would you take? Many even forgo the toothbrush and toothpaste. Would you? What's most important to you? Make

---

2. Meaning "to quit or abandon" in bikepacking racing jargon.

your list and try to weigh it. That's only the contents, you'd have to add the weight of each bag you also need to carry it in. Try it. Send us your best equipment list and tell us how much it weighs. I'd be interested to know[3] and we'll feature the most interesting lists up for other interested cyclists to check.

If participants don't take the right tool or spare parts, they may be stranded. Not enough clothes, they'll freeze; not enough food, they'll run out of energy. But now you know how much weight will affect their progress and the future will tell us if the 2020 cyclists packed wisely. And the first steep climb that will put them to the test is just ahead of them.

Back to the race

After covering 100 km of gentle hill climbs and fast-rolling terrain, the cyclists arrived at the base of Col du Portet-d'Aspet. The western slope of Portet-d'Aspet isn't only famous for its steep grade. On the way up, the final four kilometers with an average gradient of 10% have pitches above 15%. It's also notorious for the number of professional cyclists that have crashed zooming down this steep, technical, and often slippery descent. A memorial monument four kilometers before the top reminds people of Fabio Casartelli's fatal crash. He was wearing the Yellow Jersey of the leader of the 1998 Tour de France when he lost control of his bike and suffered a deadly crash on this descent. Before him, in 1973 Raymond Poulidor (French champion) abandoned the Tour de France because of a crash in that same descent. More recently, in 2018, World Champion Philippe Gilbert while racing in the breakaway, flew over the wall fracturing his knee. Pro cyclists respect and fear the steep road on this western slope whether climbing or descending it. The wet leaves covering the road can render the often-humid surface even slicker. Even climbing while standing on the pedals makes the rear wheel skid.

---

3. Contact me through my author's website: www.jpsoule.com.

Chapter 2

Yvonnick caught up to and left Chris behind on the 15% gradient three kilometers before the top.

On top of Portet-d'Aspet, I reminded participants that they'd be descending that same western slope on the way back, and should use extreme caution, particularly if the road was wet. Apart from its difficulty, the Portet-d'Aspet takes you through a thick forest, where trees hang over a fast-flowing river. Even on a sunny day, the sun's rays rarely break through the canopy, and for some, the beauty of the road isn't enough to erase the pain it takes to climb it. The descent of the eastern slope on the other side, in contrast, isn't particularly steep or technical. Yvonnick descended it with a fifteen-minute lead, racing toward what he remembered to be the next difficulty. But he had not properly studied the route.

As they descended eastward, cyclists were all anxious to climb Col de Péguère, the next iconic landmark of the Tour de France that would also be their first checkpoint after 180 kilometers on the bike. This mountain pass is mostly referred to not as "Col" but as "Mur" de Péguère. *Mur* means a wall in French. Not many climbs are qualified as walls, and as participants would soon find out, there is a reason Péguère is named so.

But, even Yvonnick, the local Pyrenees cyclist, didn't expect another climb in between. Yvonnick, a pure mountain climber, wasn't worried about mountain passes. He wasn't too much into reading maps. He had not even looked at any details of the itinerary. He was more worried about possible navigation issues and equipment as these were all new things to him, but climbing was his thing.

Just after the descent of Portet-d'Aspet, Col de la Core came as a surprise to Yvonnick. Although featured numerous times in the Tour de France, its mild gradient and a height of only 1395 meters without any particularly steep sections mean it has remained fairly anonymous compared to so many other climbs. And for many, a small bump on the map that bears the name "col" doesn't mean much. Even some 200 m hills can bear the name "col." If it isn't a legendary Tour de France climb, it's probably an easy hill that cyclists can easily race across, or so they thought.

But Chris, Yvonnick, and Pierre learned that 18 km at a 5.1% gradient, including nearly 10 kilometers above 7%, isn't just a small bump. The energy left on such a climb is energy they may wish to have on the looming Mur de Péguère. And it's very important to pace yourself and not push hard on these types of climbs.

Mur de Péguère would be the first real test of the day. It came after 180 kilometers, already more distance than most recreational cyclists ever cover in a day. And with extremely steep gradients, it promised to hurt.

It would also be the first place where novice or overly cautious bikepackers might truly pay for the weight they had packed. In a challenge featuring so many mountain climbs, each and every gram count. And no matter what book, magazine, or forums you may have read, each touting the best equipment list, packing well all comes down to experience.

Pierre, by far the youngest rider, was also much more experienced. He knew exactly the gear he needed. He wanted to be as light as possible and carried nothing that wasn't essential. Not even a tiny ultralight bivvy bag. He relied on a survival blanket but, from the beginning, he planned to make good use of hotels along the way. He was in for the long haul and believed comfort and a good night's sleep are key. Pierre's bare-essentials equipment choice, the fruit of years of experience, allowed him to start the event with a fully loaded bike barely weighting 11 kilograms.

This was experience Yvonnick didn't have. A couple of months prior to the start, Yvonnick called me to ask for equipment recommendations. I advised him on GPS, tires, clothing, lights, tools, spare parts, food, and more... And he refined his list each time we did a club ride together.

Each time, I kept reminding him of the importance of traveling light. But it doesn't matter how much you may tell a newbie in the sport. Overpacking is a mistake all ultra-bikepackers have made the first few times. You always worry about being cold, running out of food, getting stranded without the proper tools or spare parts, and most if not all first-timers pack for a heavy expedition regardless of what more experienced racers may recommend.

Chapter 2

After I told Yvonnick about essential pieces of clothing, and where he'd have to choose between comfort and weight, I recommended he test his bike with all his bags and all the gear he planned to take. First, he could not even fit all his gear in his bags. It was like playing a Tetris game, where he shoved everything in every possible direction just to try to close all the zippers and straps without any success. The first filter was that he couldn't pack more than his bulging, over-stretched bags allowed him to.

When he finally managed to close his bags, he realized that not only his bike was heavy, but that it also handled differently both in climbing and descending.

As a pure climber, Yvonnick loves to stand and dance on the pedals. But dancing on the pedals rocks the bike sideways more than sitting. While standing, he found out that his saddlebag was swinging so much from side to side that it was throwing him off balance. It also seriously hindered his climbing efficiency. Even descending was a scary experience. On tight switchbacks, at speed, his swinging bag almost threw him off the road. He not only needed to remove more weight, he needed to fix the swinging problem, something he managed to better control with heavy-duty Velcro straps.

I prefer rear saddlebags that have some type of frame or system that adds good rigidity and prevent any swinging. I find that a heavier but very steady bike is more comfortable to climb with than a lighter one that swings with every pedal stroke. But the internal or external frame that gives rigidity could add twice the weight of the empty bag. It could also be more fragile and break in case of a crash. Again, it boils down to personal choice.

After a few test rides and well-positioned straps, Yvonnick had controlled his bag to a minimum amount of swinging, but he still needed to better manage the weight of his gear.

I remember him calling me one evening a few days before the start. He was finally pleased with his gear choice and had packed it numerous times. It worked. He was happy. When I asked him for the weight of his loaded bike, he proudly replied, *"Seventeen kilograms."* I laughed loudly.

Yvonnick has a smaller build and weighs only 61 kg. He rides an XS frame bike. And he had purchased a new road bike with disk brakes especially for this event. In spite of the very functional disk brakes, his small racing bike was light. Much lighter than a larger frame bike or than a gravel bike often used on these types of events. I'm 1m83, with a form weight of 78 kg. I ride a heavy large-size gravel bike. My bike alone is more than two kilograms heavier than Yvonnick's bike. On it, I also have a heavy set of aero bars with risers, essential for the long flat distances on most events (although I wouldn't use aero bars on the Ultra Bike Pursuit.)

Despite the heavy weight of my unloaded bike and its attached aero bars, for my Oman world championship race—which, even though it included one of the toughest mountain climbs, was generally a much flatter course—I weighed my bike on the eve of the race and it tipped the scale at 16 kg. I realized it was way too much. In my hotel room, I removed all the gear that I spread over the bed and floor, and once again sorted through to try to remove anything I wouldn't need. Most of it was energy bars, kilograms of energy bars because I need to eat a lot and wasn't sure I'd find enough food through the desert. It's not a problem people would have in the Pyrenees. I started with a bike slightly over 14 kg, and that was one of the heaviest bikes out of all participants. Most others had managed to get their bike in the range of 12 to 13 kg.

It may seem frivolous to pay so much attention to one or two kilograms. After all, what difference do two kilograms make? A whole world of difference! Two kilograms on the bike is huge, as I explained previously with the example of Chris and Pierre and their fully loaded bikes on a climb like Tourmalet. Even with my empty bike weighing over two kilograms more than Yvonnick's, I would have aimed to not go over 12.5 kg with a fully loaded bike for the Ultra Bike Pursuit. Yvonnick could certainly manage to bring his to under 12 kg. But he was satisfied to have trimmed his load to 17 kg.

After laughing, I told Yvonnick the secret to packing for a bikepacking race. *"When you're pleased with your packing and all your gear, when you think you have everything you need and that all you have is essential, empty*

Chapter 2

all your bags onto the floor and remove half of it. Not the one or two items you think you may need the least. Half of it."

This means you'll only keep a small part of what you consider essential. It's sometimes a drastic choice. Sometimes it's plain impossible. This task may be the biggest challenge of all, and it happens even before you start riding. It's a constant fight in your brain as you look at all your stuff and think: Okay, can I go without this? If it's a tool or a spare part like a tire or derailleur hanger, you fear you'll break down and be stranded, unable to cross the finish because you've omitted that one piece of gear that on its own may weigh less than 200 g. But 200 g x 5 is already a kilo. Each gram counts.

How many power banks are you taking to recharge your lights, phone, and GPS? Two, that's more than a half-kilo. Are you going to ride your bike all night long, day after day, without ever stopping to recharge your power bank? Maybe one is enough. Of course, if you don't stop and ride all night long, it may not be enough.

How about food? Food is the essential fuel for long-distance cyclists. You use a tremendous number of calories when you ride all day long, and you need to eat quantities you would never imagine in daily life. As soon as you run out of fuel, you bonk, and your ride is on hold until you resupply your body with energy. And if it happens in the middle of the night, or on a Sunday when all stores are closed in France, what do you do? It's better to carry enough energy bars to ensure it never happens. Yes, but energy bars are very heavy.

In Oman, I was so worried about running out of food in the desert that I took three kilograms of energy bars. By day two, I couldn't stand biting into one anymore. I preferred the horrible junk food from the gas stations than swallowing another sweet, concentrated high-energy bar. I finished my ride with nearly two kilograms of energy bars. That's two additional kilograms I carried up the highest mountain in the desert of Oman. Stupid, but it's easy to know what you shouldn't have brought once the event is over. When you're lining yourself up at the start, you don't have all the foresight to know what food, tools, spare part, or even clothing you may need.

How will the weather be in the mountains over the next four or five days? It's impossible to predict, with each valley having small micro-climates. Will you need these arm warmers, knee warmers, rain shoe covers, and down jacket? That's a kilogram right there. Or can you do with just a single layer of rain jacket, keeping your knees and legs exposed to the cold, and let your toes go numb on a freezing descent? Will you even experience a freezing decent? After all, it's still summer and you could suffer from a heatwave, making every meter of climbing even more strenuous. So strenuous you may even consider littering by emptying half of your bags mid-climb.

Packing your bike isn't an easy affair. It's one of the toughest and most important things. Decisions, decisions, decisions.

After our phone conversation, Yvonnick said he'd go through his gear once more. But he didn't want to risk being cold. He preferred to carry a bit of extra weight and ensure his comfort, no matter how the weather would turn out. A wise decision in the abstract. Yvonnick tested his loaded bike on a couple of short hills around his house and felt confident he could handle the weight. But riding a couple of hills with fresh legs doesn't compare to 20 mountain climbs over 1100 kilometers. He started with a 17-kg bike in addition to a CamelBak water bag he carried on his back.

Enduring

Ultra-endurance bikepacking is not about racing up a mountain climb or two. It's about endurance. It's about keeping your legs working at maximum efficiency over a long period. We're not talking about six hours like Tour de France racers. We're talking about 18 to 20 hours, day after day.

Yvonnick is a climber, and although he was confident pushing fairly big gear on climbs, he at least followed my recommendation by changing his gearing from the 36-32 combination of crankset and cassette his bike came equipped with to a 33-34 set, which would not only allow him to

Chapter 2

spin more on the climbs but also when his legs got tired. With all these extra gears, he felt confident he could climb up a straight wall even with his loaded bike. And he was just about to face that challenge.

Whatever your fitness level or your endurance, every extra kilogram of body weight or gear will take its toll. Saving 10 watts on a climb can make all the difference in how your legs feel. Why do you think pro cyclists diet so drastically that many look almost anorexic? Because the extra 300 grams they can shave off their body may make the difference between the podium and a twentieth position. Weight matters.

Chris was much more versed in bikepacking and endurance racing than Yvonnick. He's very organized and had meticulously planned every single aspect of his challenge: from coaching to gear selection to route planning. He left nothing to chance. But Chris also played on the safe side of being warm in the mountains. His bike, much larger than Yvonnick's and thus heavier even without gear on, was also equipped with a set of aero bars and risers that Yvonnick didn't have. This heavy piece of equipment Chris believed to be essential, not only for the long flat sections of most events but also on any terrain, because it offers more hand positions: changing positions often relieves all kinds of pressures on your hands but also neck and back.

On his first ultra-cycling race, Chris, who had performed extremely well and was standing in the top 10 of the field, had to scratch just a short distance to the finish because of neck problems. The finish was close, but his neck was so cramped up and painful, he could no longer hold up or turn his head sideways to look around. And that's very dangerous on a bicycle.

He learned his lesson and the following year, he raced the same event with great success. Comfort on the bike is key, and for Chris, carrying the extra weight of the aero bars up the mountain was entirely worth it. His bike was also equipped with a dynamo that added weight, but it usually means you can forego a power bank. People without a dynamo will often take two power banks, Chris only needed one. Chris enjoys riding at night and not sleeping too much. And for him, using hotels is not only a waste of time, sleeping out on the side of the road next to your bike is part of the adventure that he embraces. So, he also carried a waterproof bivvy bag, a sleeping shell lighter and less bulky than a sleeping bag but that can offer good warmth by encapsulating your own body heat.

Chris carried all that he needed, but none of what he didn't. And it was acceptable for him, being heavier and more powerful, to manage a bike a little over 15 kg. Because he elected to never spend a night in hotels, he also brought a light sleeping bag, which he believed was an essential item for his goal to be entirely self-sufficient. There is nothing worse than spending a night freezing on mountains. Apart from the dangers of hypothermia, it can quickly transform your dream cycling experience into a nightmare. At age 61, Chris doesn't chase the win. He's in for the experience, and the comfort he could gain from an extra kilo of gear is entirely worth it.

Yvonnick's bike alone would be at least two kilograms lighter than Chris'. Yet Chris' loaded bike was almost two kilograms lighter than Yvonnick's. This meant that Yvonnick was probably carrying four kilograms more stuff than Chris, for someone of much smaller stature, and most likely producing less power.

Yvonnick didn't even take a bivvy bag as he had planned on doing the entire Tourmalet Pursuit Hardcore route in three days, four at most, meaning two or three nights, most of which he planned to spend on his bike. So, having warm sleeping gear, or a mattress, or a waterproof bivvy bag didn't seem essential to him. Having warm clothes to descend from a possibly cold, rainy mountain pass was important though. Yvonnick lives in the Pyrenees mountains and he knows how quickly the weather can change, and how cold and miserable it can become if you're caught in a thunderstorm without the proper gear.

I was perplexed. How in the world could Yvonnick start this event with a 17-kg bike?

I didn't know what Yvonnick had packed, but I kept wondering what he could have brought with him that was weighing his bike down so much. It reminded me of the story of the fellow that accompanied Bill Bryson on his *Walk in the Woods* on the Appalachian Trail. On day two, so burdened under the weight, he threw away most of his pack's content, including essential items such as food and even his vital water bottles. I was wondering if Yvonnick would resort to doing the same. Maybe on the very first ramp of the approaching Mur de Péguère, a climb he had long known about but never ridden.

Experienced road cyclists know that any climb above 7% is a serious challenge. When the road rises above 10%, you hope it's for a very short distance. A full kilometer averaging 10% is grueling. The difference of power necessary to fight gravity we mentioned earlier with the Tourmalet example increases exponentially with every additional percentage of incline.

Mur de Péguère is one of the short but brutal small climbs of the Pyrenees, which makes it a highlight of the Tour de France each time it is featured, and for good reasons. It is only 3.6 km long, but with an average of 12%. The average of its first kilometer is nearly 15%, with pitches at 20%. Untrained cyclists cannot climb these types of walls, even without any loads on their bikes. And even most experienced bikepackers cannot climb these grades with loaded bikes, forcing many to walk their bikes, at least for that one kilometer at 15%. In the Ultra Bike Pursuit, after 180 km, your legs aren't fresh anymore. They usually feel heavy and tired, making climbing a wall like Péguère an almost impossible task.

Walking is allowed and isn't a problem. It can even be faster than cycling on 15% slopes. It can also provide a reprieve for the legs, the different type of exercise actually letting the cycling muscles rest while you're still making progress. And sometimes, for many, it's the best solution.

Over the course of extreme mountain itineraries such as those making up the Ultra Bike Pursuit events, the repetition of big mountains will wear cyclists down, but sometimes the short and low-elevation climbs such as Mur de Péguère may tax the legs even more than a high-altitude major mountain climb. Pushing too hard on the steep slopes of Péguère could destroy your legs for the rest of the challenge.

Although Pierre is taller than Yvonnick, he's freakily skinny, though he doesn't look it because of his huge thigh muscles. Standing at 1m79 for only 54 kg makes him lighter than featherweight, even lighter than the 57 kg of legendary climber Marco Pantani.

Yvonnick at 61 kg is on par with many of the climbers who have marked the history of the Tour de France, with names such as Alberto Contador (61 kg), Nairo Quintana (58 kg), Roberto Heras (60 kg), and Joaquim Rodríguez (58 kg).

Lance Armstrong was a much bigger cyclist who in training weighed 75 kg, although it is believed but not proven, as these were secret numbers, that he lost 3 kg to line himself up to the Tour de France. But even at 72 kg, Lance was a remarkable climber because he had an incredible FTP of over 420 watts.

Even if Yvonnick managed to climb Péguère with his 17-kg load, it would tear his legs, stress his tendons and ligaments, and cause him much greater fatigue than if he had an 11-kg bike like Pierre.

First checkpoint

I drove past Yvonnick on the gradual climb that led from the village of Massat to the intersection that would lead to the wall. I didn't wait for him anywhere on the climb and drove straight to the top. I feared that my wide van would take too much space on this narrow road when Yvonnick may need to swerve his bike around to fight the grueling grades.

Yvonnick reached the top with a big smile… and a little swearing.

"That was a really mean climb," he told me as he stopped after the two flags I had set up to celebrate everyone's arrival on top of the first checkpoint.

Yvonnick had the proper gearing for it, and he really appreciated having changed his small ring to a 33 and his cassette to boast as many as 34 teeth that allowed him to spin his legs on the steepest sections. He didn't even litter the climb with any of the content of his overloaded bike.

But he said, *"Tell Pierre that if he's able to climb this wall on his 34-28 with a loaded bike and without walking or setting foot on the ground, he's a beast."*

Yvonnick was the first participant on top, reaching the 180-km mark at 18:04 in exactly 10 hours. That was an 18 km/h average over a mountainous itinerary with a heavy bike and including all bathroom, food, and rest stops. His riding, moving pace was thus much faster. That was very fast. Could he keep this up to the end? Or was he riding the Ultra Bike Pursuit as if it were a single-day ultra-event? Would his muscles seize tomorrow or the next day?

At this point, Yvonnick felt great. On top of Péguère, he confided that he was hoping to finish the ride in three days. I didn't want to say anything that could lower his confidence. But distances are deceptive. The first 200 kilometers, in spite of the steep sections of Portet-d'Aspet and Péguère, included proportionally less elevation gain than the remaining course. If weight management is the most important thing in the planning stage, pacing is the most important thing while riding, that and managing your sleep and rest time.

Although I was on top of Péguère for each participant, the official checkpoints were self-monitored. When they arrived, participants needed to take a selfie picture of themselves with their bikes and the sign of the checkpoint and send that on a WhatsApp group monitored by both the organization and all participants. As Yvonnick took his selfie, distant thunder made us wonder if Chris and Pierre were cycling under a storm. A thick fog was quickly moving in and Yvonnick zoomed down toward Foix as I waited to greet and cheer the others.

An hour later, just after 19:00, Chris reached the top of the wall and took a breather. He might have been sweating profusely, but he was dry, at least on the outside.

Less than two minutes later, a soaking wet Pierre crested the top with a huge smile and before I asked anything, said, *"I loved it!"*

I asked if he had any trouble with his gearing.

"Not at all," he replied.

Pierre, like Yvonnick, loves climbs more than anything else. He's a pure climber. Even though he doesn't define himself as a *rouleur* (a strong cyclist on the flat), the young man works as a bike messenger in Lyon and can carry huge loads, sometimes a fridge or washing machine. All that furniture hauling probably helped him crest Péguère with gearing too high for most cyclists to stay on their bikes on such a climb. Even Yvonnick wasn't sure he could have managed Péguère with a 28 cassette, hence his previous comment.

Chris, who was only wearing a jersey and a pair of light arm-warmers, quickly put on a rain jacket. Pierre was already wearing his because of the downpour he faced minutes before the climb. They chatted as I took photos of them next to the sign. On this forested pass, the evening light combined with the thickening fog quickly decreased both the visibility as well as the temperature, and both were on their way down less than five minutes later.

The next landmark on the map that our cyclists were looking forward to was the legendary mountain pass of Port de Pailhères. Pailhères is the first climb above 2000 meters on the route, and is the tallest mountain of the French Eastern Pyrenees. It's been featured numerous times in the TDF and is known as much for its length and difficulty as it is for its perfectly carved, tight, picturesque switchbacks. To cyclists, Pailhères sounded both like a scary challenge and a dream of a climb. Challenge and beauty often go hand in hand.

But again, Yvonnick had quickly scanned the route separating Péguère from Pailhères without paying much attention to the 100 km separating them. When you look at the chart of an elevation profile spread over a long distance with mountains higher than 2000 meters, hills don't even show and many smaller climbs appear insignificantly small as if they were gentle rolling hills.

A good descent took them to cross the town of Foix, an important stop to fill up on food[4] and supplies as there wouldn't be much later on if they decided to ride into the night.

Managing your food is an important part of bikepacking.

---

4. The self-sufficiency rule means that participants aren't allowed to receive food or any other supplies from friends or family during the event. They must carry with them all that they may need, but they can purchase anything from any commercial venue available to all participants.

⛰ Nutrition

The purpose of this book isn't to serve as a training guidebook or nutrition plan, but it is important to understand how the body uses fuel to move forward and to recognize how fuel affects endurance athletes.

Energy, hydration, and electrolytes are the three components of nutrition. The athlete's fuel (source of energy) is food. The three main macronutrients in most foods are carbohydrates, proteins, and fat.

Sports nutrition books always list carbohydrates first, because it's the most important source of energy, which is why it requires a little more information and I'll save it for last.

Proteins are essential to building tissue. They are the major component in enzymes and hormones, and are sometimes even used as an energy source. Some proteins are produced by the body; other essential ones need to come from food intake. They can be found in some legumes and particularly beans, but animal meats have the largest quantity and higher quality of protein. Plant sources often lack essential amino acids. Soybean is the exception, as it provides a rich amino-acid protein comparable to that of animal protein. Vegetarians need to eat a wide variety of vegetables to ensure they intake all the essential amino acids, which is why many choose to supplement their daily diet with plant-based protein powders (e.g., made from peas or flax and pumpkin seeds).

Because of the constant stress on muscle fibers produced by ultra-endurance efforts, it's essential for athletes to eat a sufficient amount of protein for them to repair and maintain those fibers. However, although essential, protein isn't a real source of energy during sports (even though a small quantity of amino acids can be transformed into glucose, its negligible).

You may think that fat is your enemy. For decades, the media and public opinion have waged a war on fat. But it's important to distinguish between body fat (which, when left uncontrolled, leads to obesity and all the derived health problems) and the essential fat nutrient. Eaten in a reasonable quantity, fat is not only good for you, it's vital. Fat is the source of the fatty acids that the body cannot produce. It helps with the prevention of colds and other infections common among athletes (because they may not have enough body fat). It prevents dry skin and hair, and it helps women maintain a regular menstruation cycle. It also helps the body absorb the fat-soluble vitamins A, B, D, and K, which can only be digested and used by the body with the aid of fats.

There are four major dietary fats in the foods we eat: saturated fats, trans fats, monounsaturated fats, and polyunsaturated fats. Saturated and trans fats are bad for health. Monounsaturated fats and polyunsaturated fats can lower bad cholesterol levels and are beneficial when consumed as part of a balanced diet.

For ultra-endurance athletes, an important piece of information is that fat is the body's most efficient source of energy. Each gram of fat contains nine calories[5]. One gram of fat yields more than twice the amount of energy provided by one gram of carbohydrates. A simple deduction would be that energy-starved endurance athletes could consume a significant amount of fat to sustain their effort. Wouldn't that be great? But it's not that simple.

The body stores fat as a source of energy. So all athletes, even lean ones, have a significant level of energy stored as fat. An 80-kilogram athlete with 10% body fat has 8 kilograms of fat, storing 72,000 calories. A more sedentary person with 20% body fat has twice as much energy reserve. It sounds great to think that the fatter we are, the more energy source we have—but here is the catch.

Adenosine triphosphate (ATP) is the primary carrier of energy in cells. But to convert a unit of fat to ATP takes a longer time and requires more oxygen than it does to convert a unit of carbohydrate. Because this process requires more oxygen, thus the higher your heart rate, the more you're tax-

---

5. A calorie is either of two units of heat energy: a small calorie (cal.) is the energy needed to raise the temperature of 1 gram of water by 1°C (used primarily in physics and chemistry); and a large calorie (Cal.) is the energy needed to raise the temperature of 1 kilogram of water by 1°C (used to measure the energy value of foods in food science and nutrition). Thus, a large calorie is equal to 1000 small calories and is also called a kilocalorie (kcal). For the purposes of this book, the energy value of foods will be expressed in calories and sometimes be abbreviated as Cal.

ing your oxygen level, the less your body is able to convert fat into ATP, and the more you have to rely on carbohydrates to provide you with energy. And because it takes much longer for fat to convert into ATP, it isn't as readily available as carbohydrates. But the body doesn't store nearly as much glycogen (energy from carbohydrates) as it does fat, so fat is of particular importance to ultra-endurance athletes.

For decades, coaches and sport medicine scientists recommended that endurance athletes consume high percentages of carbohydrates, up to over 80% of their nutritional intake. But for physical efforts lasting longer than four hours, and particularly for ultra-endurance athletes, recent studies showed it may be beneficial for them to consume 30% to 40% of their energy source from good fats. This would be splendid news if good fat, like those found in vegetable oils (except palm oil) and fish, were readily available during events. Everybody should avoid saturated and trans fats, but the problem is that most of the processed foods found in gas stations (which sometimes are the only places open when cyclists reach a town at night) are rich in these bad saturated and trans fats. One of the worst choices are the potato chips so many endurance athletes crave during efforts because they are salty. They contain a high concentration of saturated and trans fats and are best avoided. It's not the type of calories you want to fuel your body with. Some of the best sources of good fat that cyclists could easily transport with them are dried nuts, particularly almonds. Athletes who regularly train at low intensity teach their body to burn fat more efficiently. They use a higher percentage of fat instead of carbohydrates to produce the energy needed during efforts. This helps them save their glycogen reserves (energy from carbohydrates) for longer periods of time.

Carbohydrates are the main source of energy and are particularly important for endurance athletes. One gram of carbohydrates yields 4.2 calories. Although it's only half of the energy produced by one gram of fat, it's readily available energy that can be quickly transformed into ATP without taxing too much of the body's oxygen. There are two types: simple carbs and complex carbs.

Simple carbs, also known as simple sugar, have one or two molecules of sugar, and include glucose, dextrose, and fructose. They break down quickly in the body and can be used by the muscles to be transformed into energy. Simple sugars are found in fruits, vegetables, milk, refined sugar, candy, and soft drinks. The body doesn't store these simple carbs. What it doesn't use right away, it transforms into fat to be stored for later use.

Complex carbs have three or more molecules. We find them in pasta, rice (preferably brown), potatoes, grains and cereals, whole-wheat bread, bananas, berries and other fruits (fresh, dried, or even canned), plain yogurt, and more…

The body stores complex carbohydrates as glycogen in the muscles and liver. This is a readily available source of energy that the body can use during efforts. The problem is that stored glycogen reserves are limited. That same 80-kilogram athlete may have about 500 grams of glycogen, although it can be boosted a little more by eating a carbohydrate-rich diet. Muscles will store 400 of these grams, and the remaining 100 grams are stored in the liver, for a total of 1,600 calories. That's 45 times less energy than the 72,000 calories stored in fat (or more if the person has over 10% body fat). It represents a very small quantity of energy that can be quickly depleted during efforts. The faster your heart rate (or the higher your power zone or heart rate zone), the quicker you'll deplete these glycogen reserves.

But here is something particularly interesting for endurance athletes to consider. Carbohydrates are not digested. They are transferred from the stomach to the bloodstream through osmosis. Osmosis is the movement of water from a solution with a high concentration toward a solution of lower concentration (the concentration here being carbohydrates). Water is the transport vehicle for these nutrients through osmosis. The problem is that there is a limit to the amount of water your body is able to absorb.

As your muscle burns more energy, your blood cells keep sending it fuel. When you ingest an isotonic drink (which has a carbohydrate concentration similar to that of your functional blood cells), as you deplete your blood cells of sugar, the carbohydrate concentration from the isotonic drink in your stomach will filter through to your bloodstream to re-establish balance. But if you take a hypertonic drink (which has a higher sugar (and/or salt) concentration than that of your functional blood cells), because the sugar concentration will be higher in your stomach, it will absorb water from your bloodstream to dilute this sugar (and/or salt) until it reaches balanced osmosis between your stomach and blood. This is bad, as it momentarily dehydrates you and could cause all kinds of stomach pain, gas, and other issues. Only when the balance is attained will the energy from this hypertonic drink transfer to the blood vessels in your muscles. It may seem counter-intuitive, but this is what happens when you swallow an energy gel. Its high sugar concentration will create an imbalance between your stomach and your bloodstream, using the water from your bloodstream to dilute it. It can create many undesirable effects in the middle of a long endurance race. This is why it's best to always drink water each time you take an energy gel or any type of high-concentration energy bar.

You may wonder why I'm explaining this: Because the osmosis between the stomach and the bloodstream is based on the concentration of the number of cells in the solution, not the size of these cells. Simple carbs have only one or two molecules of sugar. They are very small particles. Complex carbs have more molecules of sugar. They are larger particles. When the same number of particles are exchanged between the stomach and your bloodstream, a solution with complex carbohydrates will transport about twice the energy of a solution with simple carbs. The number of particles transferred is the same, but the amount of energy each particle is made of is much higher for complex carbs. This is why endurance athletes who need a constant supply of energy should favor foods and drinks with complex carbs over those with simple carbs.

How do you know the ratio of complex versus simple carbs within foods and drinks? Look at the packaging's nutrition label for the total amount of carbs and under it for the amount of sugar. If the number of grams of sugar is equal to the number of grams of carbohydrates, then 100% of the carbohydrates are simple sugars. If you get 3 grams of sugar for 10 grams of carbohydrates, it means you're getting 7 grams of complex carbohydrates. If you divide the sugar by the total number of carbs, you get the percentage of simple sugar versus complex carbs. You should favor products with 30% or less simple sugar, or 70% or more complex carbs.

A quick food and sports summary: The main source of energy comes from carbohydrates. Complex carbs are more efficient and preferred to simple sugar. Fat also makes a great source of energy for ultra-endurance athletes, but it requires more oxygen and takes longer to be transformed into energy. The body can use a higher percentage of its energy from fat when training at a low-cardio intensity. Trained athletes are more efficient at converting fat into energy. But there are bad types of fat you should stay away from: saturated and trans fats. Proteins are essential for many things, and of particular importance to ultra-cyclists to rebuild muscle tissues.

Even though electrolytes and hydration don't provide any energy, they are at least as important as food.

Hydration is by far the most important aspect of nutrition. Yet most people in their daily lives aren't drinking enough water, which is even more true during physical activities and a frequent problem especially in endurance sports. A very simple formula applies not only to endurance athletes but to everyone else: the more dehydrated you are, the less you will perform. If you wait until you feel thirsty to drink, it's too late.

The recommendation from the American College of Sports Medicine is to drink between half to one liter of water per hour (16 to 32 ounces) during exercise. Standard bike water bottles hold approximately half a liter. Unless it's a very hot day, many cyclists go on four-hour rides without drinking more than the content of their two water bottles, which means they drink less than a quarter of a liter per hour, half the minimum recommended amount. They may double that amount on hot days, but it's still half of the recommended water for exercising in hot weather.

Athletes often don't know they are dehydrated. It's best to assume that anytime you do a sustained endurance effort over multiple hours, you most likely won't be drinking enough on a regular basis. Your body will be dehydrated whether or not you are consciously feeling it. The more you can reduce this state of dehydration, the better you will perform.

Dehydration can lead to cramps, muscles and tendon injuries, and many more problems. As a general rule, most endurance athletes don't drink enough, so drink as much as you can, and never wait to be thirsty.

You may wonder if there is a risk of over-drinking. We're not talking about alcohol here; we're still talking about water. Yes, there is a risk called hyponatremia, which occurs when the concentration of sodium in your blood is abnormally low. Sodium is an electrolyte that regulates the amount of water that's in and around your cells. When the sodium in your body becomes too diluted, your body's water levels rise and your cells begin to swell. This swelling can cause many health problems and even become life-threatening. However, it's very rare for athletes to suffer from hyponatremia. It usually happens when athletes over-drink many liters of water hours before their event. They drink so much that they urinate all the time, and through their urine they lose all their electrolytes. Sodium and other electrolytes are the keys here. But to be at risk you'd have to force yourself to drink incredible and possibly uncomfortable amounts of water prior to an event, which would have you urinating a lot. Athletes shouldn't worry too much about hyponatremia and drink as much as possible during their effort. As mentioned, in most cases, and particularly in hot weather, athletes won't drink enough to stay properly hydrated.

A great tip for cyclists in France: Many villages have water fountains. The sign "Eau Potable" confirms that the water is safe to drink. But even when there aren't any fountains or any shops open to fill up your bottles, most villages have cemeteries, generally found next to or behind the church. And all cemeteries have drinkable tap water.

The importance of sodium leads us to look at minerals, or electrolytes. Electrolytes are positively and negatively charged ions that conduct electrical activities to perform various functions within the body. Electrolytes must be present in proper concentrations to maintain fluid balance, muscle contraction, and neural activity, which are all essential not only to high performance but also to basic daily functions.

We've just mentioned the vital property of sodium, but the body requires 21 essential minerals, including sodium, calcium, potassium, magnesium, chloride, iron, and zinc. It isn't within the scope of this book to list them all, but here are the basic roles of some of these minerals:

Calcium is essential for bones, teeth, secretion of hormones, and enzymes. It also plays a role in muscle contraction and nerve conduction, which are of capital importance to endurance athletes.

Iron is a key component of hemoglobin, a protein in your red blood cells that transports oxygen in the blood. It's also a component of immune functions.

Zinc is an essential part of hundreds of enzymes in the body and is important for proper cellular and immune functions.

One issue that athletes face with minerals is the low absorption rate of the body. But that low absorption rate is also a blessing, as it makes toxicity due to an overdose of minerals very rare. Plainly said, if you swallow too many electrolytes, your body will ensure that eventually you'll flush that excess down the toilet.

Sweat is produced to cool off the body. Athletes, and particularly endurance athletes, sweat much more than non-active people because physical activities produce a high amount of energy and heat. The hotter the body gets, the more it will produce sweat to regulate its temperature. As well, the hotter the environment, the hotter the body will get, and the more you'll sweat. Even though sweat is a fantastic thermo-regulator, it is not without its problems. When sweating, you're losing not only water but also all the essential minerals. This is why athletes shouldn't only drink a lot of water while training or during an event; they should also replenish the precious electrolytes they lose through their sweat.

One last bit of information about sweat in hot and very humid weather. The actual act of sweating isn't what cools off your body. Cooling happens when your sweat evaporates from your skin. Energy is required to turn liquid into gas. Your body heat is the energy source, so when your sweat evaporates, it takes your heat with it. When it's hot and the humidity is high, the air is already saturated with moisture, causing this evaporation process to slow down or stop—leaving you drenched and uncomfortably hot. The hotter the air, the more moisture it can hold. This explains the images we've seen of the many distressed competitors during the 10,000-meter women's run of the Tokyo Olympics. It was a particularly hot and humid day. Gold medalist Sifan Hassan needed much time with her body covered in ice packs to recover enough to stand up after her incredible win. Many others couldn't cross the finish line. They had trained in hot weather, but the high humidity made it particularly challenging.

Although many of these minerals are found in all kinds of food, quantities of electrolytes from food may be insufficient to balance the loss athletes experience during long endurance efforts. This is why it's highly recommended to take electrolytes supplements. The hotter the weather, the more supplements athletes may need. Most energy drinks are also filled with electrolytes. But energy drinks often have a high sugar concentration. The more dehydrated you get, the more sensitive your stomach may become (see the explanation about osmosis transfer between the stomach and the bloodstream).

Personally, when I start to become dehydrated, I can no longer swallow any sweet fluids, and I can't bear to eat anything sweet either. The more dehydrated I get, the less I can eat. Beyond a certain dehydration state, even salty food becomes unbearable. This is a problem, as there is no more energy without food. It's a catch-22 because dehydration often occurs during a prolonged effort that also depletes our body from energy. We need to stay hydrated, but we also need to regularly eat enough calories to sustain the effort. I've tried dozens of energy drinks, and my stomach just can't handle any of them, even those from companies that swear their product is easy on the stomach. My solution is to only drink water while I'm exercising. I'll have juice or energy drinks when I take a few minutes to stop and eat something. At a lower heart rate, my stomach seems to handle sweet drinks better, but not while I'm riding.

The problem is that I'm highly susceptible to cramps and I need a regular intake of electrolytes to help prevent them. Instead of taking electrolytes in a liquid form in my bottles, I take pills. I find them more efficient, and much easier to swallow when dehydrated, than any electrolyte drink. Another great advantage is that they are easy to take at regular intervals. It allows me to fill my bottles with only water, which I drink easily, even with an upset stomach, and thus without any restraints. I would never enter an ultra-cycling event, even in cold weather, without a good reserve of electrolyte pills.

Food is the athlete's fuel. If you planned a car trip from the United States to Panama, you'd fill up your sports SUV with the highest quality fuel. You'd find decent fuel in Mexico, but from the time you enter Guatemala until you reach Panama, you'd have to settle for poor quality diesel that has been cut so many times you'd wonder how vehicles still run. Your SUV will run, but certainly not as well as it did when you were crossing the States.

The same is true for food. Athletes usually eat a well-balanced diet throughout the year. They avoid saturated fats (potato chips, processed food, etc.) and ensure they have no vitamin or mineral deficiencies. It's so important that, in many sports, pro athletes and teams travel with their nutrition specialists and chefs. That's particularly true for multi-day cycling events such as the Tour de France or Giro d'Italia.

The problem ultra-cyclists face is that they can't carry enough food to supply all the calories they burn. And they often have limited choices of what is available. They may reach a town at night or during closed business hours. They may have no choice but to purchase what's on offer at the local gas station or on the side of the road. Sometimes they are lucky to find a supermarket with a great variety of choices. But other times, there isn't much. And stopping in restaurants is too time-consuming for ultra-cyclists.

Another problem is that digesting good food isn't easy during efforts. It's even harder when you eat a lot of junk food. Apart from saddle sores and skin rashes, one of the most common ailments ultra-cyclists experience is stomachache. Many things could upset your stomach: from not digesting something well, or eating something you aren't used to, to stomach acid, or gas, or many other reasons. And even with good food, your stomach can play tricks on you when you get dehydrated and really hold you down. Sometimes a stomachache can even force you to stop.

Chapter 2

I will never forget an experience in Oman, over the first 500 km, when the only supplies were from gas stations: sugar-covered fried donuts, potato chips, and similar food. I was craving something salty, but there was nothing. I usually like potato chips, but I couldn't bear to even look at them. The thought of eating these greasy items felt appalling at the time. I only fed on my energy bars. In the morning, when I saw a few cyclists eating some burgers and fries, I immediately joined them. It was the most disgusting burger I had ever eaten. I'm not sure what the meat was, but it didn't taste like meat. Luckily, there was ketchup to cover the taste. I quickly swallowed a few bites until the taste fully registered. Though I really needed more food, I couldn't finish more than half of it. I ate all the fries though, and off I was back to riding through the desert, still dreaming of a real salty meal.

In the Pyrenees, cyclists have less to fear. Most villages have bakeries, with an assortment of salty and sweet delicacies. There are plenty of supermarkets and restaurants everywhere, including many that will serve quick sandwiches, omelets, or even salads. We eat well in the Pyrenees. The problem is timing. Restaurants only open a few hours for lunch and dinner, and they usually close around 21:30. Bakeries close for a couple of hours at lunchtime, and early in the evening. Supermarkets sometimes don't open until 9:00 or 10:00, which is very late for ultra-cyclists. So if you plan to stop in a town late in the evening to check in to a hotel for a few hours, sometimes you may have to choose between checking in to the hotel before they close or getting dinner somewhere. That's if you don't arrive too late—you may end up out of luck both for finding food and a place to stay. To make matters worse, most shops are closed on Sunday, and even sometimes on Monday. Not stopping when you have a chance, because you want to ride farther or think you don't need anything yet, could prove to be a costly choice that you'll pay for a few hours later.

Local specialties

Luckily for our cyclists, from the first checkpoint of Péguère it's a short downhill to the town of Foix where they can have a hot dinner, and a chance to taste a local *cassoulet*, *confit* or *magret de canard*, or even a *garbure*.

Cassoulet, a rich, flavorful casserole of white beans slowly baked with a combination of meats, is a specialty of France's southwest regions. Its origin is uncertain, but a legend from the town of Castelnaudary claims that it was created during a British siege of its castle during the Hundred Years' War (1337–1453). The story goes that the starving French put all the food they had left into a single dish of beans with a mixture of lards, pork, poultry, and sausages—and this rich food combined with the local wine so invigorated the soldiers that they chased the English back to the north of France. At least starving cyclists know what dish they can eat to gather the energy they may need for their long battles up the road.

Although the most famous *cassoulet* comes from Castelnaudary, there are two other variants, one from the UNESCO World Heritage fortified medieval town of Carcassonne, and the other from the Red City of Toulouse. All three cities, located less than 100 km from each other and all in the vicinity of Foix, claim to have the original dish.

Historians believe that the root may actually come from the 12th-century Middle East, but the entire region of southern France has refined it to make its own signature—a must-eat meal for all visitors. *Cassoulets* take their name from the *cassole*, the earthenware dish in which they were traditionally cooked, and come in many versions. All three use the regional specialty of duck *confit* to which they add pork and bacon in Castelnaudary and Carcassonne or sausage in Toulouse. The first dish was made with fava beans, but the local white varieties of beans have replaced them. Other variants use mutton, which may have been the original meat used in the Middle East.

Quality and taste vary tremendously from one restaurant to another and recipes can be as simple or elaborate as the chef desires. Canned versions of varying qualities and prices are also sold in supermarkets. It's delicious, but not a light meal; it has all the calories starving ultra-cyclists crave.

If you don't find *cassoulet* in all restaurants, almost every town in the Pyrenees will serve you *confit de canard*. This dish, made of goose or duck meat slowly cooked then preserved in its own fat, is common in the Pyrenees and Gers regions. It is exquisite accompanied with *cèpes*, a gourmet French mushroom; *Tarbais*, the famous Tarbes white beans; or even plain potatoes. *Confits* are served as a main dish but also used in other French culinary specialties such as the delicious Pyrenees *garbure*.

I know what you're thinking: I just mentioned problems linked to some types of fat, and particularly animal fats, and now I highly recommend duck cooked in its own fat! The duck magic doesn't stop with its fabulous taste, however. Unlike most land animals, and more like fish, the duck's fat is rich in mono-unsaturated fatty acids (omega 9) and is healthy as part of a balance diet. Duck fat is much healthier than butter, and many people in France use it for cooking instead.

If you aren't an endurance cyclist and try to stay away from all fats, even the good ones, duck meat is a good choice as it's lean (less than 190 calories per 100 grams) and rich in many essential nutrients such as phosphorus, iron, zinc, selenium and vitamins B1, B2, B3, B6, B12 and E. You might enjoy a steak of duck, which you'll find served in restaurants all over the southwest of France and Pyrenees under the name *magret de canard*. I love all red meat, of which duck is my favorite—it tastes better than beef and is much healthier too.

Garbure is a rich bean soup, usually made with *confit de canard* or *camayou* (boned ham) and seasonal vegetables. It's cooked all day long until it becomes thick, sometimes as thick as a light stew. No two cooks make their *garbure* exactly the same way as it is traditionally based upon whatever ingredients are available. In small villages, farmers still practice a custom called *chabrot*, where the leftover broth from the soup is mixed with the equivalent of half a glass of red wine right into the bowl and then drunk. Local restaurants serve *garbure* as a full meal or as a starter (a lighter version of broth with vegetables only). Ultra Bike Pursuit participants may not want to do *chabrot*, but after a rainy, cold day they'd be especially delighted to dine on *garbure*.

Along with duck *confit*, these are some of the dishes cyclists on my tours can sample, along with a dozen more regional and local specialties. After a good day of cycling, we treat ourselves to a few cold beers, a massage, jacuzzi or pool swim, a copious meal to sample all the best food of each valley, and some of the best wines. It's often too much food, but when dessert arrives, it's impossible to resist the masterpieces set on our plates. It is with a full belly and a few shots of local spirits that we collapse in our comfortable hotel rooms. It'd be decadence if you didn't deserve it, but we call it cycling in style and I have to admit that I love it. I love the hardcore ultra-bikepacking as well. They are two different approaches to cycling, each offering a wonderful and unique experience.

If they don't stop in Foix, I hope participants will have the chance to try some culinary specialties during their event, because one of the numerous pleasures of cycling is to be able to eat all the delicious food you desire, and the Pyrenees offers as many specialties as it does mountain passes. Now let's go back to find our ultra-cyclists and see how they planned their evening meals and sleep.

The first night

It's still a long way to Port de Pailhères, and considering that many shops in small French villages are closed on Monday, Yvonnick and Chris may have made a mistake by not stopping in Foix to resupply.

Pierre had closed the gap on Chris on the Mur de Péguère, but prior to that ascent he was still kilometers behind, and under what he described as a deluge of a thunderstorm. Cold and drenched to the bones, he stopped for the day and checked in to a nice warm hotel in Foix.

Pierre understood the difficulty of the full itinerary. He wasn't competing with Yvonnick and Chris, who were both riding the 1100-km course. He planned to cross the finish line of the 2300-km Ultimate Pyrenees Pursuit within the 12-day deadline. He understood the importance of resting well at night, something that wouldn't be possible sleeping in the open without a bivvy bag when he was already wet and cold. A hotel night, a shower, and a chance to dry his clothes was the best thing he could do to ensure the success of the rest of his trip.

There was a little friendly competition between the two older men, who almost matched each other on the bike on this first day. The hour separating them was nothing. The difference, they knew, may not be made on the bike, but in managing the rest stops, and particularly their sleeping times.

The two men had ridden at a similar speed for the first 100 kilometers. Chris, taller and heavier, was more powerful. With his triathlon aero bars and power, he had the advantage on the flat and had been leading on the earlier rolling parts. Yvonnick had the advantage on the climbs, which meant an overall advantage on this course.

But Yvonnick lacked experience in bikepacking events. He stopped often, and always for too long. He kept looking for things, forgetting where he had stuffed such-and-such piece of clothing or gear. He always had to empty his entire bag on the road to access his gloves or reflective vests, wasting precious time, over and over, while Chris was methodical, well organized, and very efficient, limiting his stops to as few and as short as possible. There was no fussing around looking for jackets or food when needed. Chris knew where everything was. He had planned all his gear to be instantly accessible.

Yvonnick was wasting time on all the stops he made to buy food and eat, and for nature calls. Every stop that Chris managed in two to five minutes seemed to take Yvonnick 20 to 30 minutes.

I know how it feels. When racing across Europe, my wife was as organized as Chris, didn't need to eat or drink much, and never wanted to stop. She kept complaining about how often and how long I was stopping, and I hated to admit that she was right. Then, when I raced in Oman, after a mechanical problem stranded me at the back of the race from Km 100 and I spent a full night passing people, the next morning I passed a charming lady who was in contention for the female podium. After we talked for a few minutes, I resumed my pace, much faster than hers. I stopped to go to the bathroom, then flew by her again. I was riding on the flat at 40 km/h, while her pace was probably around 30 km/h, and you'd think that we might not see each other again, but it proved to be a great illustration of the Jack Rabbit fable. I stopped to fill up my bottles in a shop but without finding much to eat. It took me a full half an hour to catch up to this lady who never stopped. Twenty minutes later, I saw a few participants having a hot lunch of burgers and fries. Desperate to get something salty I joined them, ordered the same, and had started eating when she arrived. She also ordered the burger and fries, yet didn't stop longer than 10 minutes. When she resumed riding, I was still having a drink and finishing my food. She had arrived 10 minutes after me and left 10 minutes before. Even with speeds as drastically different, we spent hours playing yo-yo. It was only after half a day when we climbed the first long gravel mountains that I took a lead she didn't close. I didn't manage my stops well at all, and remembered how much I disliked my wife telling me so, but she was right. It was something I had to improve on for the rest of the race. I remembered one of my friends mentioning the randonneurs' first mantra, *"If the wheels are not turning, you're wasting time."* I learned from my mistakes as I was forced to recognize that managing stop times efficiently was more important than riding fast.

Yvonnick too would have to reduce the time he wasted on every stop, but there was another very important moment when one could gain or lose much time.

Managing sleeping time may be one of the most important components of an ultra-endurance challenge. It's a compromise between sleeping well and wasting as little riding time as possible.

A nice hotel room is without a doubt the most comfortable option. But it comes with a few drawbacks. First, it may take time to reserve the hotel, check in, and make the payment at the reception of a busy hotel. I remember on our race across Europe sometimes wasting as much as 30 minutes for the busy or lethargic hotel reception staff to check us in and take my payments. That's 30 minutes less of sleeping or riding time, 30 wasted minutes miserably standing in a lobby when all you want to do is collapse into sleep.

Having a hot shower is fantastic, but that's another half an hour spent doing things other than the essential sleeping. I know what you're thinking. A shower doesn't take half an hour. But it does, or at least your time in the bathroom does. In hotels, cyclists often take advantage of the room to wash their laundry and set it up to dry overnight. They sometimes also wash or wipe their bikes, oil the chain, and do some basic maintenance. It's much more comfortable to do all these things in a warm hotel room than it is in total darkness while wasting the battery of one or your precious lights.

Most ultra-racers who choose to stop in a hotel usually check out in the middle of the night after a few hours of sleep. But when an appealing breakfast incites you to stay a little longer, you may gorge yourself on precious calories for the day's ride, but the quick night stop that you thought would only be three to five hours, may suddenly extend to seven or eight. That's seven hours off the bike, during which you may have only slept four hours. You will always sleep less time proportional to the amount of time you've stopped in a hotel than on the side of the road.

Pierre thought it was wise to take the time to be well rested on his first night after being drenched. But Chris and Yvonnick chose to sleep on the side of the road to minimize their stopping time. They didn't stop in Foix, not even to resupply on food, probably a mistake. They moved on and continued to ride with the firm intent of reaching at least Port de Pailhères, which was the second checkpoint at Km 306, and descending to the other side before catching a few hours of sleep.

Reaching the other side of Port de Pailhères was the minimum Chris had originally planned to accomplish on his first day. Covering 350 kilometers on a first day isn't unusual in bikepacking events. But the base of the Pailhères climb still loomed 86 km ahead of Foix, and the night had already dropped its curtain.

Immediately out of town, the road elevated itself to yet another unknown climb most cyclists didn't expect, although the road led to the historic site of the medieval Cathar castle of Montségur. History fans would know that all Cathar castles in the Eastern Pyrenees were set on the tallest hills to make them difficult to attack. And although the 2.5% average gradients were mild, it was a 30-kilometer climb from Foix to reach Montségur, but it wasn't a col marked on any map. And on the chart of such a long ride profile, it's easy to not pay attention to roads that look almost flat, either because they are long-low-grade climbs, or because they are very short in distance even though they may be steep. But 30 kilometers up, even with a low gradient, will take the best out of you when you've been riding non-stop for 16 hours.

Most mountain climbs on the itinerary offer stunning mountain views, but what makes cresting this climb remarkable is the view of Montségur. Under the auspices of the Catholic Church, the crusaders, in their effort to exterminate the Cathars, not only assaulted and sacked their castles but tore most to the ground, leaving nothing but their foundations. Very few Cathar castles still stand today. But Montségur is one of the best preserved, most beautiful that has survived through time and is currently on the list with seven others to become a UNESCO World Heritage Site. Although parts of it are in ruins, thousands of people flock from around the world to visit it.

It was around 22:00 when Yvonnick first set his eyes on the illuminated chateau. He was tired and needed to lie down for a well-deserved rest. He found a shelter soon after the chateau and stopped for a few hours. Sticky wet, sweaty, and smelly, he drifted into a profound sleep. The hard cement floor he had to sleep on with no mattress was a tradeoff in comfort for shelter with a roof in case of rain.

Chris reached Montségur at around 23:00 after an impressive ride, but also with the understanding that he had underestimated the difficulty of the itinerary and that the daily distances he had covered in other bikepacking events were simply impossible to cover on the Ultra Bike Pursuit. He passed by Yvonnick's sleeping spot to find his own a few kilometers farther.

After using wet wipes to wash up and changing into a set of merino base layers, Chris settled clean and dry into his lightweight sleeping bag on top of an ultra-light inflating pad and wrapped inside his waterproof bivvy bag for a warm and comfortable sleep. Yvonnick didn't have the luxury and comfort of a pad and sleeping bag, or even a bivvy bag. He didn't plan on sleeping much and chose not to carry such gear. He relied instead on the paper-thin and light mandatory survival blanket, along with some warm clothing to sleep a few hours. If he'd had a bivvy bag, Yvonnick could have chosen a soft grassy bed as a more comfortable option.

Sleeping outside in your dirty cycling kit without a padded mat or sleeping bag isn't the most comfortable, but when your body reaches a state of physical exertion you may have never previously experienced, it's surprising how quickly you can fall asleep, and even, possibly, how well you may sleep. That all depends on the spot you find, but when your body tells you to stop, and body fatigue dictates the distance you can cover in a day, you may not have much time to be picky, and although experience helps in picking the best spot, luck often determines the quality of your rest stop. After riding over 235 kilometers, the two men slept less than five kilometers apart.

Chapter 3

On the Way to the Mediterranean Sea (September 7)

Yvonnick had barely stopped for three hours, during which he said he slept less than two hours, when he resumed cycling at 02:45.

The descent from Montségur took the cyclists through quiet rural roads followed by more climbs than they had expected such as Col de la Croix des Morts, Col des Sept Frères, Col de Marmare, and Col de Chioula, before a short descent that would take them to an intersection three kilometers above Ax-les-Thermes. The official Pailhères climb starts from the town of Ax-les-Thermes. Arriving from Chioula, cyclists can hop on the climb and skip its first three kilometers.

It's after 291 kilometers that they attacked the 15-km ascent to the top of Pailhères. If the 7% average seems mild, the gradient gets steeper over the last 10 kilometers, and even steeper over the last five that approach a grade of 10%.

The Pyrénées-Orientales share a distinctive characteristic with all the regions bordering the Mediterranean Sea: they are often exposed to strong winds. Pailhères, the last Ariège climb standing at 2001 m above the Mediterranean, was a perfect shield for the valleys that lie west of it, but upon reaching its top you're exposed to the strong winds from the coast. Even though you can't yet see the sea, the mountains ahead are much lower, allowing for the gusts to hit you at full strength and head on as you climb

Chapter 3

the last kilometers to reach the top of Pailhères from the west. This can sometimes make this climb even tougher.

It was while fighting strong headwinds that all three participants pushed through the last kilometers to the top.

Yvonnick arrived first on top at 08:40. Usually, morning winds are the mildest, yet he reported strong, challenging winds. At least, the cloudy sky from the previous day gave way to blue and he could glance in anticipation at the next mountains he would climb under a bright warm sun.

Chris had resumed his cycling at 04:45 after four hours of good sleep from his five-hour stop. He reached Pailhères at 11:40, a remarkably small gap of only three hours separating him from Yvonnick after over 300 kilometers of mountain cycling. If, on these events, your only competition is yourself, the presence of other participants within a reaching distance is a great motivator and something you can monitor as a dot-watcher. A three-hour difference can quickly be made in many ways. A small mechanical incident, a sudden lack of energy, or simply the need to sleep a little more.

Yvonnick had not yet covered half, not even a third of his course, and anything could still happen. There was still no guarantee that he would be able to cross the finish line. Without the experience of multiple days cycling ultra-distances, maybe he had started too fast, not slept enough, and had already eaten into his energy reserves and taxed his body much beyond what was necessary. Maybe he would pay for it.

Behind in Foix, after a good shower, drying all his clothes, and having a good long night's sleep in a warm bed, Pierre resumed his riding at 07:00. He was probably still sleeping on his bike, though, as it was 10 kilometers into his morning ride that he realized he had left his helmet at the hotel. What's a small 20-kilometer detour with a mild climb when you're taking on 2300 km? At least, his 10-hour stop served him well, and although he was already seven hours behind Chris, Pierre had the experience to listen to his body. It's important not to push yourself to a point that you won't be able to ride efficiently on the following days. Finishing the full Ultimate Pyrenees was not the sole goal for Pierre. He wanted to do so while enjoying every single part of it. He wanted to see all the wonderful scenery. He wanted to feel good on the bike. Resting well at night was for him a priority.

A priority that certainly paid off, as he reached the top of Pailhères at 13:40, only two hours behind Chris, having thus already closed five hours of his morning gap in a mere 100-kilometer distance. And that was after taking the time to stop on top of the first hill to marvel at the sight of Chateau de Montségur. Pierre stopped everywhere along the way to take photos. He had never ridden the Pyrenees before and wanted to record all of its beauty.

By noon, Yvonnick was riding the 32-kilometer mild climb of Col de Quillan under a scorching sun to reach the mountain village of La Llagonne, marking the start of what all cyclists would later describe as a spectacular route. Another three kilometers of steeper climbing took him to the top of Col de la Llose, and then followed a fabulous descent on a narrow twisty corniche dug out into the cliffs.

The Pyrenean would later say: *"I had never heard of this climb, but this small road led to one of the most incredible descents I had ever done."*

Pierre later told me: *"The mountain views, the narrow canyon, and the deep plunging cliffs, on this extremely narrow road free of any cars, was one of my most amazing experiences."*

After that 23 kilometers of magical descent, when it merges with the main road, the descent continues for an incredible 56 kilometers, a treat that ends less than 40 kilometers from the coast.

Historical rest stop

Descents can be thrilling, but long ones can cause neck pain. A 20-kilometer technical descent can be exhausting. The more relaxed you remain on your bike, the easier it is, but over time all descents take their toll.

The first section from Col de la Llose descends 23 km on a narrow road carved into cliffs all the way to Olette. It's a technical one, but a small price to pay for what Pierre may remember as the best descent of his life. When reaching the main road, cyclists still have 31 km of downhill before taking a turn onto a side road. This descent never ends, it seems. But there is no better place to relax your neck and your hands from the aero position and constant grip than the medieval village of Villefranche-de-Conflent, conveniently located 9 km after Olette.

Most cyclists may fly by it, not knowing what hides behind the sight of the fortified walls. If they take the time to look above the ramparts, however, they will notice, high up on the hill, a seemingly impossible-to-reach castle overlooking the entire valley, well protected by its surrounding geography. They may wonder how people access this improbable fortress.

 Villefranche-de-Conflent

The ninth-century village of Villefranche-de-Conflent has long been on the official list of the most beautiful villages of France, and was a favorite tourist destination for over a century much before its 2008 UNESCO World Heritage recognition gave it an added boost. This prestige will ensure locals will continue to preserve the village without any modern constructions to disrupt the old-stone harmony of the superb traditional church and houses that make it a must-see destination.

This site was first occupied by the Celts, then by the Romans, Visigoths, Muslim Moors, and the Spanish, a reminder of the rich history of all the Pyrenees regions. But it was during the ninth century that the counts of Conflent built the first fortifications around what was at the time the local capital and a prosperous trading town. The Spanish captured it in the mid-1400s and added defense weapons to the fortification. After the French took it back in 1654 and their 1659 signing of the Treaty of the Pyrenees, the town became a strategic location to stop possible Spanish incursions.

Vauban, considered the greatest engineer of the 17th century, was an architect and the trusted military engineer of Louis XIV, France's most famous king, also known as the Sun King or the Great King. It was Vauban who replaced the old fortification with the current walls and 10 years later added Fort Liberia, a castle built barely 800 meters from the village, but 400 meters higher.

Vauban fortified hundreds of towns and erected castles all over the country, as the Great King had a vision to make France the greatest and most powerful country through a series of wars and treaties. The greater his military and technological power, the more he'd be able to control Europe and assert his domination over the forces of the neighboring British, Dutch, and Spanish, the other established empires at the time. He greatly expanded the French colonies into Africa and sent explorers to claim new lands all over the world. It was under his mandate that in 1673 French explorers discovered the Mississippi River and continued to expand French territories as they moved upriver until they reached the Gulf of Mexico. They claimed the Mississippi basin region in Louis' name, calling it Louisiane—now known as the US State of Louisiana.

Vauban was afforded unlimited funds and resources to give France a strategic advantage to ensure victories even against the combined forces of all its neighbors. France at the time was known for its military power and the merciless cruelty and arrogance of its king. Louis XIV spent his entire life building Versailles, a palace to his image, one fit for the greatest of kings, the only one after God, the Sun King; a wonder to show France's glory and supremacy which would remain as the most famous legacy of his reign. Vauban was one of the few key people the Sun King had entrusted to make France the greatest country of all.

It took decades to complete Vauban's construction plans to fully fortify the village and finish the castle. The construction of this fortress started around the same time as that of the citadel of Mont-Louis located at the top of the valley, less than an hour by bike from the Spanish border. The original Ultra Bike Pursuit itinerary looping into Spain returned to France at the foot of the citadel. The modified route won't permit participants to set their eyes on another of Vauban's masterpieces, all the more reason for them to return next year. But not to worry, there is plenty for them to see in Villefranche.

Chapter 3

Cyclists with tired legs may not want to climb the steps linking the village to the castle through the tunnel that Napoleon III had later built between 1850 and 1853. Nicknamed *"Le Souterrain des 1000 Marches"* (one thousand steps underground), even though it only numbers 734, it is not only the longest set of underground steps in France and one of the longest in Europe, but each was sculpted in beautiful pink marble from the region. There was no tunnel during Louis XIV's reign, and accessing the castle was so nearly impossible that he used it as a political prison—or in other words a family prison, since at that time, most of Europe's powerful leaders were family members by blood or marriage.

The castle wasn't only a place to seek safety or protection; or maybe it was, but mostly for the protection of the Great King himself. The 17th century was a time when your worst enemies weren't those you were waging wars against but those closest to you, and poison was a more powerful weapon than cannons to eliminate those in your path to a great position and fortune.

Between 1677 and 1682, many prominent members of the aristocracy were implicated and sentenced for poisoning and witchcraft. The frequent killing of nobles with what became known as "inheritance powders" led to a flourishing underground trade of deadly concoctions. Historically known as the Affair of the Poisons, it was recently brought back to life in the *Versailles* TV series. Thirty-six people were judged and sentenced to death, but hundreds of people were suspected. In the midst of this affair, the king was terrified of being poisoned, an obsession exacerbated by the fact that among the accused were a few of his ex-mistresses.

Miss Des Œillets, who had mothered a child the king refused to legitimize, and the Countess of Soissons, herself a former mistress of the king, were convicted. Des Œillets was none other than the court's companion and assistant to the official royal concubine, the Marquise de Montespan, with whom the king had legitimated his relationship and all the children they had together.

Although the Marquise was not suspected by the king or the police, her name was on everybody's lips. She was even suspected by the court gossips of killing the king's new mistress, although history would show it was a natural death and that she had committed no wrongdoing whatsoever. The 36 people found guilty were killed or imprisoned for life. A long period of witchcraft hunting followed. If a court conviction was necessary for public executions, mere suspicions were often enough for people to disappear.

The king and his advisors deemed it necessary to take precautions and dismantle all the poison network. Louis XIV had two suspects, the Marquise de Brinvilliers and a lady known as La Chapelain, detained in the fortress above Villefranche. From the top of Fort Liberia, you may enjoy the beautiful view that was theirs for 36 and 43 years respectively until their natural death. Although this period of ruling above any laws gave the Sun King some peace of mind, it didn't help his image among the French nobility and people.

Before giving birth to her seventh child with the king, the marquise was replaced by her younger long-time friend and confidante, whom she had given the position of royal governess to raise the king's children. Françoise d'Aubigné, later known as Madame de Maintenon, would become the king's last concubine and subsequently his uncrowned wife. She also became the closest advisor to the Sun King. She is the one who influenced him and his police to put a stop to the frequent and unexplained disappearances. Her aim was for the king to regain some of his image, tarnished by his authoritarian and cruel handling of the poison affair.

Cyclists who are not too grizzled by their never-ending descent and strong desire to reach the Mediterranean Sea may relax their necks and delight in strolling through narrow cobblestone streets and among half-timbered houses to eat at one of the many restaurants or enjoy a fabulous rest at one of the cafes, while happy tourists browse the small art galleries, boutiques with lavender-scented crafts, and eateries specializing in local sweets. Luckily, life in the modern-day village is much more pleasant than during the 18th century.

And, if you can escape from your *donjon* cell, you can enjoy a trip aboard the *Train Jaune*, as Villefranche is its starting location. Although the railway linking the coast to the upper village of Prades reached Villefranche in 1885, it wasn't until 1909 that a special mountain railway was built to link Villefranche to the Mont-Louis citadel, and then to the Spanish border through Latour-de-Carol in 1911.

The Villefranche-Mont-Louis leg is a marvel of engineering as the narrow railway crosses through 19 tunnels and two impressive suspension bridges overlooking 65 and 90 meters of emptiness as the "yellow train" switches from one side of the canyon to the other and back. Other railroad sections seem to cling to the sheer cliffs. Visitors or tired cyclists will enjoy the ride (you can take your bike on the train) and the views without having to climb 60 kilometers, but you won't go much faster than a strong cyclist, with a top speed of 30 km/h and no less than 22 stops in villages, it takes three hours to link the two UNESCO World Heritage sites, but the slow excursion is an experience on its own.

Although the train is yellow because it's touted as a tourist attraction, it is a regular passenger train that is part of the national railway system, with real connections to other destinations and a short shuttle to connect you to the international train line taking you directly to Barcelona, or to Toulouse if this is where you started your trip.

As you board the train, you may wave at our participants that zoom down the road, often overlooking the yellow wagons. But even if you're descending with the train, don't expect to see our participants for long: they'll fly by the train at over 50 km/h on the superb asphalt and zoom by the *Train Jaune* as if it were frozen in time like a glorious vestige of the past.

There is so much to see, but with so many kilometers to ride, cyclists can't stop to visit it all; they need to keep pushing on the pedals, whether it's up, or down. History abounds in the Pyrenees. After a short pause at a Villefranche cafe to reflect on the people who've seen these same stones over the centuries, I'd better catch up with our cyclists, because they continue racing to write their own history.

Final dash to the Mediterranean Sea

Continuing on that long descent straight to the coast would see increasingly heavy motorized traffic with more trucks and fast driving cars on a dull road. Such unpleasant road sections were purposely not featured on the itinerary. Instead, the route takes a right turn on secondary roads.

It's psychologically tough to know that the gradually descending road you're riding on is the most direct way to the coast and that you could reach the beach in less than an hour. As you make a right turn on quiet roads, a quick look at your itinerary will inform you that you still have to ride 70 kilometers to reach the coastal town of Collioure, the third checkpoint. And these 70 kilometers aren't flat. A small price to pay to cycle these wild, rugged, rural roads.

It was mid-day when Yvonnick reached that turn, certain that he would arrive on the coast by early afternoon. After all, 70 kilometers of rolling hills couldn't take much longer than two-and-half hours for a trained cyclist.

Meanwhile, Chris was having a very different sort of day.

That morning on the Pailhères climb, Chris had run out of food. It was a Monday morning, and after the town of Foix where he didn't stop, none of the shops in the small villages were open. Chris bonked. That's when your muscles are depleted of all glycogen energy. Unless you eat enough calories, your body runs on basic survival mode, only converting energy from fat. Your legs feel extremely heavy, your whole body is tired, and you can't put any pressure on the pedals. As you ride painfully slowly, it feels that you're making no progress. A two-hour climb suddenly transforms into a four-hour "Via Dolorosa." Your brain plays tricks on you. Each pedal stroke costs you more than the previous one. It takes a very strong mind not to give up. Chris kept riding at a pace he managed to sustain until he could find some kind of food.

In the back, a well-rested Pierre, who had already closed a four-hour gap by the time he topped Pailhères, had continued his fast progression, enjoying every moment of it, and particularly loving the Col de la Llose.

Chapter 3

With still relatively fresh legs and in good spirits, Pierre took the right turn on secondary roads. It was only a matter of minutes for him to catch and drop Chris, only 10 kilometers ahead. But that didn't happen.

Looking for a place to fill up his water bottles, Pierre met a friendly couple who invited him to their house. At 20:00, even before nightfall, he sent me a text: *"I'm stopping for the night. People invited me to their place."*

The young man rides in style… Another night with a shower, a warm comfortable bed, as well as real food. And he followed up with this text message:

"One of my most beautiful days on a bike in my entire life. Really.😄😄😄"

Chris reached the right turn by the end of afternoon, and trailing Yvonnick he continued toward the Mediterranean Sea on these secondary roads.

After that turn off the main road, the cyclists quickly understand that the additional distance isn't the only thing that will eat into their time to reach the coast. The road slowly winds up the first hill, and the silky-smooth blacktop surfaces of the Hautes-Pyrénées are behind you. Many secondary roads in the Pyrénées-Orientales are covered in chip seal asphalt and not maintained as often as they should be. The most experienced ultra-bikepackers know how to ride on these while conserving a maximum amount of comfort and energy. They use wider tires inflated at low pressures.

Even road cyclists on smooth roads have recently moved to wider tires and low pressure. Riding on over-inflated 23 tires is something of the past, old school, even though many amateurs still ride 25-millimeter-wide tires at high pressure. Decades ago, scientists believed that higher pressure tires offered a lower rolling resistance and were thus faster. Recent studies show that a lower pressure, although in theory generating more rolling resistance, often does not negatively affect speed, particularly on rougher surfaces. A rougher road surface being defined as anything other than a smooth road as sleek as the track of a velodrome.

Higher pressure on rougher roads means that the tire is jumping up and down at the microscopic level, and losing grip on the road. This loss of energy compensates for any gain on rolling resistance offered by high pressure inflated tires. Also, a lower pressure tire offers more cushioning. It absorbs all the micro-vibrations, and even smoothens the bigger bumps, holes, and other irregularities of the road. Modern tires are extremely efficient, and even with width as much as 28 or 32 millimeters and fairly low pressure, they offer a surprisingly low rolling resistance.

A wider tire inflated at low pressure offers a significant amount of additional comfort: comfort that cyclists feel instantly as they ride, but also comfort at the microscopic level, by absorbing the micro-vibrations that cyclists may not be aware of or even consciously feel, but that take their toll by adding enormous fatigue at the end of the day.

Yvonnick, who had covered the first 400 kilometers of Pyrenees mountain roads at an incredible speed and with relative ease, was suddenly struggling on these small Pyrénées Orientales roads. It wasn't because his legs were tired, but it was the constant bouncing on the bike. He described these rolling hills as bumpy and tough.

Yvonnick was riding on 28 wide tires, a good tire width for this course, although 32 would have been more comfortable. I didn't understand why a light cyclist like Yvonnick should have suffered so much on this 50-kilometer section until I talked with him after the ride. He had inflated his tires with an 8-kg pressure (115 PSI). Even for road cycling, that was old school. It was the kind of pressure we put into 23 tires 20 years ago. Tire technology and width have changed, and so has research. It was no wonder 50 kilometers of rough roads destroyed Yvonnick's body much more than all the climbs he had done.

For a man who weighs only 61 kg like Yvonnick, the best tire pressure for these roads with 28 tires would have been 4.2 kg (60 PSI), 70 PSI at the very most, as he was using traditional tubes instead of tubeless. I would have ridden the entire course on 32 tubeless tires inflated at 60 PSI but that's because, at 78 kg, I'm 17 kg heavier than Yvonnick. With 32 tubeless tires, Yvonnick could have ridden with a 55 PSI pressure for maximum efficiency and a much greater level of comfort. That's half the pressure he was using.

Chapter 3

With the correct pressure, the bumpy rural roads of the Oriental Pyrenees would have been much smoother. Not buttery smooth like our backyard roads in the Hautes-Pyrénées, but much more comfortable. The high-pressured tires he rode on conducted all the vibration through his entire body. With half the tire pressure, Yvonnick would have instantly felt more comfort in his hands and arms, and a lot less fatigue from the micro-vibrations. It was a lesson Yvonnick learned the hard way. But he isn't the only one to make this mistake. Most cyclists I know, whether they are my friends in France or the majority of my tour customers from the United States and Australia, over-inflate their tires by huge margins like I still did a dozen years ago.

At 17:55, Yvonnick reached the third checkpoint at Km 482, just in time to admire the picturesque harbor town of Collioure and fix a flat tire with the last rays of the sun still illuminating the medieval fortress reflecting in the water of the small bay. He resumed his ride into the night after sending us his mandatory selfies, proof that he reached the checkpoint.

After eating some food, a rejuvenated Chris had started to cycle that road section that had taken the best out of Yvonnick. But Chris, although much heavier, was riding 30-mm tires with a pressure of 75 PSI, a much lower pressure, and he certainly suffered less from that road section than Yvonnick had. After a hot afternoon, Chris probably also enjoyed the cooler night temperatures.

While Pierre was relaxing and Chris was making good progress toward Collioure, Yvonnick faced further challenges in the Oriental Pyrenees.

Only 72 kilometers on mostly flat and good surface roads separated Collioure from the entrance of the Galamus Gorge, the base of the first climb leading back to the Central Pyrenees. Theoretically, for a rider like Yvonnick, that was less than three hours away, a distance he intended to cover before sleeping.

But after his tough time reaching Collioure, and fixing his flat, Yvonnick was tired, and his struggle wasn't over. That coastal section was exposed to strong winds.

Yvonnick may not be quite as light as Pierre, but they share the same forte: climbing. And like Pierre, Yvonnick does not fancy flat roads exposed to strong wind. After two hours of fighting the wind and barely covering 35 kilometers on flat roads, an exhausted Yvonnick collapsed into sleep at 22:00 on the side of the road in the village of Thuir.

The next day, he told me that riding against the wind was the toughest thing he'd ever done, worse than climbing multiple mountains.

Chris made it to checkpoint 3 by 23:15. Unlike Yvonnick, he felt good and didn't waste time. He immediately continued. His extra weight, superior power, and handy aero bars were all great attributes on this flat and windy section. Chris continued riding into the night until nearly 01:00 and found a good sheltered spot to lie in his bivvy bag for a few hours of rest. After two full days of riding, a mere 35 kilometers separated him from Yvonnick.

Chapter 4

Pailhères, the Oriental Giant (September 8)

At 02:00, Yvonnick sent me a text. He was up, packing, and almost ready to resume riding. Almost ready means less than two minutes for Chris, but that's another half an hour for Yvonnick. He sent me another text 25 minutes later saying he was about to leave, which probably meant that after he packed his phone and finalized getting ready, another 10 minutes flew by. It was still a short four-and-a-half-hour stop, during which he probably got no more than three hours of sleep. That made it a total of six hours' sleep over the first two nights after riding two monstrous days. Yvonnick would later tell me that when he stopped for four hours, he would get less than two hours' sleep. That it always took him the longest time to find the best spot, unpack his bags, change his clothes, get ready to sleep, and he would waste as much time once he woke up repacking everything before finally being ready to set off.

I wondered, *Could Yvonnick continue riding at this pace, on so little sleep?* He'd barely covered half the distance, and not yet 50% of the elevation.

It was before sunrise that he climbed through the deep Gorges de Galamus without being able to enjoy the views from the narrow road carved into the cliff. By 08:40 he was at the base of Port de Pailhères, the Giant of the Oriental Pyrenees, this time to climb it from its eastern slope. The day before, Yvonnick had swallowed the western climb as if it were a small rolling hill, but the eastern climb is utterly different: equally challenging, but with scenery that shows the clear distinction between the regions of Pyrénées-Orientales and Ariège which the col borders. A set of superb tight switchbacks leads cyclists up to an open meadow with free-roaming cows and horses. On top, following the mountain ridges, majestic Pyrenees vultures with a 2.4-meter wingspan soared effortlessly.

I was on top for sunrise, enjoying the view over the distant mountains, and the stately ballet of the soaring vultures. I waited for the arrival of Yvonnick and Chris. Knowing Yvonnick's climbing abilities, I had estimated that as he started his climb at 08:40, he would reach the top before 10:15.

I waited to take photos as a bright and gradually hot sun forced me to remove my jacket, and made me sweat, even though I wasn't riding a bike.

I waited, always at the ready to take photos. And waited longer and longer. Yvonnick never appeared. I kept checking my phone to see where he was on the dot-watching satellite map, but although there was a phone signal, there were no satellite signals, which meant he was still toward the bottom where the valley is too deep to let any signal go through. Did he bonk? Was he paying for his riding too fast on his first day?

Pain

It was not until 13:24 that Yvonnick crested the summit. He had stopped numerous times, suffering from his Achilles tendon. Already the previous day, he had developed huge blisters on the back of his heels. It was painful, but a pain he could live with. But the Achilles tendon was more serious, and a problem that could force him to quit.

Two kilometers before the top, as I took his photos, Yvonnick said, *"I'll make it to the top and maybe scratch from the race. I can't take the pain."*

On top, he showed me his shoes. He had cut a huge piece from the back of both his shoes as to not make any contact with his tendons or even the back of his heels. That helped, he said, but the Achilles tendon pain was still unbearable.

It was Km 744, and 53h20' into his race, and I could read immense fatigue on Yvonnick's face, maybe amplified both by the added pain and his less than optimistic feelings. He looked like a broken man ready to quit.

A person can fight muscle pain. In fact, apart from serious repetitive cramps that could tear muscles, there is no level of muscular pain experienced in endurance efforts that the mind cannot overcome. But tendons and ligaments are different. It's not that they are more painful, it's that unlike muscular pain, they usually keep worsening, and could then cause permanent damage. All athletes know this, and after a certain point fighting that pain no longer makes sense and you have to accept that abandoning is the only solution. What bothered Yvonnick most, though, is that apart from his Achilles tendon, his legs otherwise felt great. But his spirit started to wane as he saw his dream of being a finisher slowly vanishing; he wasn't ready to quit yet, but he understood it was likely.

He knew that from the top of Pailhères, he could freewheel the 17-kilometer descent to Ax-les-Thermes, with another 26 kilometers of gradual downhill all the way to the town of Tarascon. That was over 40 kilometers where he wouldn't have to put any pressure on the pedals until he reached the start of Col de Port.

"I will push to Tarascon and reevaluate there, whether I can continue or need to quit," he said before rushing down the hill.

Yvonnick would have to fight pain and all his demons to be able to finish. When you reach this level of suffering, only your mind can take control over your body. Yvonnick would have to dig deep into his mental strength, and hopefully, his body would follow.

Chris had resumed cycling at 05:40 and arrived on top of Pailhères by 17:25. Only four hours behind Yvonnick, Chris looked great. He looked even fresher than the previous day, and our conversation confirmed that he was feeling good. A huge contrast with the disheartened and suffering Yvonnick. Chris looked as though he was on a short club ride. He paced himself to perfection, relying on his years of experience.

It was hot when Yvonnick descended, wearing only his short-sleeve jersey. Thick dark clouds had now moved closer to the mountain and im-

Chapter 4

mediately sent the temperature down to a cold chill. Chris hurried to put on his jacket and head down the mountain to avoid a possible downpour.

It was a very laid-back Pierre who started riding late in the morning, after enjoying a good breakfast kindly offered by his hosts. Pierre checked in at the Collioure checkpoint before 11:00, almost a full checkpoint behind Yvonnick. But when Pierre rides, he rides fast. And although he said he wasn't strong on the flat and into the despised wind, he devoured the flat sections. He started his day later and almost 100 kilometers behind Chris, so imagine my surprise when I noticed his satellite beacon nearing the base of the Pailhères just as Chris was heading down.

Pierre crested the top of Pailhères climb at 19:35, just two hours after Chris departed. It was incredible. Despite stopping in various places in the Galamus Gorge to take photos that he sent us, he had once more closed an almost 100-kilometer gap.

But sometimes a two-hour difference can lead to an entirely different experience. Chris, after enjoying some food in Ax-les-Thermes, was racing after Yvonnick toward Tarascon.

When Pierre arrived on top of Pailhères, the sky suddenly fell on him, dumping a curtain of water so thick he could barely see the road. Between poor visibility and a lack of braking power, as Pierre used old-style caliper brakes, he took longer to descend the mountain than he had taken to ride up it the previous day. Before the end of the descent, in pitch-dark, soaking wet and cold, he stumbled upon an open auberge in the small mountain village of Acous. A gift from the God of Thunder, who after dumping his fury on him took pity. At least, a welcome relief for him to dry off and spend another cozy night as his fellow cyclists continued riding. It made for yet another early stop for Pierre, who had called it a day by 20:30, but what a day it was.

Yvonnick, after some ibuprofen and loosening his legs on the long descent and flat section, felt much better. The pain from his Achilles tendon became manageable. As the pain dulled into an ache, his spirit quickly returned and he was more driven than ever as he pushed forward.

He quickly rode up to Col de Port and ascended the 1264 m Lac de Lers, reaching it at the time Pierre reached Pailhères.

Lers lake is at a low elevation where many mountain valleys would be covered with thick forest, but centuries of cattle and sheep herding have left wide green pastures with patches of trees here and there, and open mountain views. The five-kilometer climb leading to Col d'Agnes offers superb views of the lake as the road winds through rock gardens. Before the top, your ascent is accompanied by the musical rhythm of dozens of bells from cows grazing at the side of the road. There are no sharp peaks on this northern climb, only rounded mountain tops and a thick velvet tapestry of green. It's the peaceful serenity of the place on this rarely used narrow road that gives it all its charm. When Col d'Agnes comes into sight, the golden granite towers of Mont-Ceint summit stand in contrast to the gentle rolling meadows.

Yvonnick arrived on the top of Col d'Agnes before sunset, when the light from the sinking sun bathed the mountains in an orange glow. I met him as he reached the top and stopped to put on his jacket, saying, *"This is an incredible climb! So close to home and I had never ridden it. I loved it. I have to come back here."*

It was only upon asking him that he said the pain had mostly gone, and that his legs were feeling better than ever. Achilles tendon pain doesn't disappear like this with a couple of ibuprofen pills. He had won the battle of the mind over the body.

And that was a good thing because the next climb, though only 5.9 kilometers long—too short to look more than an insignificant bump on the general elevation profile—was a bump with a 7.5% average gradient. A bump that had a full kilometer at 14%. The type of bump that hurts when you have fresh legs and no load to carry. And Yvonnick didn't even know it was coming up. It was a bit of a shock, after descending with a stunning sunset that enveloped the dark mountain contours with a light burgundy red, when minutes later he had to stand up on his pedals into the night to fight 14% slopes.

Chapter 4

Col de Latrape would never be just a bump anymore to Yvonnick. Its altitude might only be 1112 m, but this should be a reminder to cyclists that it isn't the highest mountain passes that hurt the most, and that the lower Pyrenees mountains have no reason to envy the Alps for they host more climbs, more diversity, and more challenge.

On top, Yvonnick lost track of time, or even of what he was doing. He was obviously tired, not thinking clearly as he unpacked his bag under the beam of a streetlight as there are habitations on the low altitude Col de Latrape. He spent minutes looking for something, forgetting what it even was. When he remembered he was looking for his neck warmer, to cover his throat for the descent into the night, it took another 10 minutes emptying all his bags and searching for it everywhere before he realized that he had already instinctively put it on around his neck as soon as he had stopped. He laughed, repacked all his gear, and was finally ready to descend.

It should have taken Yvonnick two minutes to put his warm clothes on. Five at the very most, even if he was not well organized and had to empty his entire bag again. It took him 25 minutes to do so. When you reach this level of tiredness, when your mind isn't clear, not only do you not have the energy to push on the pedals, which makes your riding inefficient, but you are no longer lucid enough to ride safely. It's time to stop. And this is what Yvonnick did as soon as he was down the mountain.

Although Yvonnick had originally wanted to push another 35 or 40 kilometers before stopping to sleep, the tiny Latrape had been one climb too many.

Revising your goals is something you must do regularly on these types of events.

On a public bench under the roof of the town hall next to a river in the village of Seix, wrapped in his survival blanket, Yvonnick fell asleep before 23:00.

Chris pushed on another hour, allowing him time to climb and descend Col de Port. Before midnight, he found refuge in a small village on the way to Massat.

Exhaustion

There are various types of physical exhaustions. Some are muscular, where you've pushed too hard on your muscles and depleted all your glycogen; this is what endurance athletes call bonking, what happened to Chris on day two, and is probably the most common in endurance sports. And luckily it is the least severe, for your body usually forces you to stop before you endanger yourself. And it's also the easiest to recover from with a good meal and some rest.

You could also experience exhaustion from heat and dehydration that could be accompanied by cramps, nausea, head spin, imbalance, and even vomiting. It's a very serious condition that could eventually lead to a coma and death.

You could have exhaustion from hypothermia, when your hands and feet are so cold that after going through various pain levels, you lose sensation. And the more you get numb, the less you can control your bike, the less you can squeeze your brakes. It can then be accompanied by shivering, so strong it may shake your bike and throw you off balance. It could continue with a general drop in body temperature. These symptoms can happen any time the temperatures are cold, but it's even more frequent when you descend a mountain. After a good effort climbing and sweating, your soaked body suddenly doesn't require more effort to descend, and no longer produces the energy that kept you warm on the climb. The wind from the descent adds to the cold temperatures. The more fatigued you are, the more sensitive you are to the cold.

This state is also dangerous. Suffering from freezing fingers and hypothermia, shivering, you are no longer lucid and able to react quickly and control your bike.

I remember once on a very hot summer day, Yumi and I were climbing to the Pont d'Espagne in the National Park. Not a single cloud broke the uniformly blue sky. It was 38 degrees Celsius and I was suffering from the heat. I hadn't brought a jacket, not even a light shell. When it's this hot, the less I carry on a climb the better. After we made a brief stop to admire

Chapter 4

the waterfalls, the clouds moved in quickly, and the suffocating hot and humid temperature dropped in minutes to a near-freezing level. As thunder and lightning surrounded us, we were surprised by a downpour so violent we couldn't see two meters ahead. There was no fog, it was just the heavy rain. This was before disk brakes and we had lost all braking power. My wife had been smart: she was carrying a light jacket, which, although not fully waterproof, gave her some protection against the wind. Still, she was freezing.

Ten kilometers into the descent with almost as many kilometers to go, in my short-sleeve summer jersey, I was so cold I started to suffer from hypothermia. My full body was shivering so hard, I had to stop in the middle of the deluge, certain I had broken or at least bent my wheel because it was sending me all over the place, and without proper brakes, it was dangerous. I checked my wheel. It was perfectly trued. Nothing abnormal. I resumed cycling down and again felt I was going to crash because of my bike shaking all over the place. That's when I realized that it was my uncontrolled shivering that was being conducted into the bike. Even though I had not reached a serious level of hypothermia requiring immediate medical attention, I learned that being cold on a bike is not only extremely uncomfortable. It's plain dangerous. And a further drop in body temperature can even lead to more serious problems, coma, and death.

I learned from my mistake, and even on hot days I always pack a lightweight waterproof jacket to ride in the mountains. And I fully understood how happy Pierre must have been to find that open auberge after his cold, wet descent of Pailhères.

But both heat exhaustion and hypothermia are usually avoidable by using proper equipment, proper food and fluid fueling, and by managing your efforts and using common sense.

Stopping to go faster

There is one more type of exhaustion that generally does not affect most recreational endurance athletes. It's more specific to the extreme long effort of ultra-endurance athletes. That's sleep deprivation.

When you undertake a multi-day challenge such as an ultra-bikepacking or ultra-trail event, the clock does not stop until you cross the finish line. Often the amount of sleep isn't regulated and you can push your body as long as you wish or can. And often the stronger you are mentally, the more you will push yourself.

If many people can cope with an entire sleepless night, most start drowsing on events longer than 36 hours unless they stop and get enough sleep.

The physical demand of long hours in the saddle takes a lot of energy and requires even longer resting time for your body to heal and operate efficiently. Sleep is not essential, it is vital. But unlike muscle exhaustion, as you dive into various levels of sleep deprivation, your body doesn't ache. Unlike heat exhaustion or hypothermia, there aren't many clear warnings. Of course, you feel tired. But that's normal when you spend 18 to 20 hours on your bike day after day. Ultra-endurance athletes are used to that state of tiredness, and they are so mentally strong that they constantly push their limits further. But it's easier to fight muscle pain than to stay awake; after all, it's just pain.

When your body can go no longer, falling asleep usually happens very fast. It's not something you can fight forever, even with the strongest of mind. The first signs are general fatigue, but we all continue through this. General fatigue can come from many things, even lack of food, and is considered a normal state at many given times in an ultra-endurance event. Everybody experiences it. But past a certain level of sleep deprivation, your eyelids just drop their curtain, and there is nothing you can do about it.

You can fall asleep in a second. And falling asleep on a bicycle isn't a good thing. The most likely outcome is an instant crash.

The questions then become: Where are you going to crash? Are you on a flat country road with a nice field of wheat bordering the road that will cushion your fall? Or will you suddenly cross the road to find yourself facing a speeding truck? Or maybe you are descending a mountain pass with a tight switchback and a 100-meter-drop cliff from which you'll plunge to your death.

These aren't just farfetched worst-case scenarios, they are real, plausible results of falling asleep on your bike. And the chance of you falling asleep while descending a mountain is even higher than while climbing it. Because as long as you climb, you put energy in your pedals, your heart rate is higher, you may even be in a little physical pain, all these things help you stay awake. As soon as you crest the top and plunge into the descent, your body relaxes, your heart rate decreases. You lose your concentration, and it doesn't take long for your body to shut down, forcing you to sleep. And when you're descending a mountain, arriving at full speed into that turn over a deadly cliff, it could be the end.

Athletes who haven't done multi-day ultra-distances may not comprehend this, but there is nothing harder than fighting sleep deprivation. When it comes, no mental strength can help you keep your eyes open. Even deep pain can only give you a few additional seconds of alertness before you slumber. You can deliberately cause yourself pain by biting your tongue, your lips, your fingertips where they meet the nail, you could even slap yourself on the cheeks until you look like a lobster. This will only gain you seconds, minutes at most before you fall asleep again. Falling asleep is unavoidable. Every ultra-endurance athlete has experienced these levels of sleep deprivation, and many ultra-cyclists have crashed because they haven't stopped when they should have, thinking that their mental toughness could fight it, or because they didn't even feel it coming.

It happened countless times to Yumi and me during our full crossing of Europe. We pushed for 33 days of long hours on the bike with an average of barely four hours of sleep per 24 hours. I nearly died once when I fell asleep in the descent of the Alpine pass of Petit-Saint-Bernard taking me from Italy to France. Luckily a huge bump in the road jerked my front wheel and the shock woke me up seconds before my front wheel touched the rail guard. I would have flown over the cliff to take a deadly dive.

Another time in Andalusia, on a gentle descent, I closed my eyes to wake up only when my front wheel was stopped by a rock sending my rear wheel up into the air to perfectly line up vertically with it. Flying into the air, I didn't have time to be scared. All I could see was the desert bush I was going to land on. Cactus and thick thorns, or not? Luckily it wasn't, and I didn't hit any stones. I still got a contusion on my right IT (iliotibial) band that hurt me for the remainder of the race. I was in a lot of pain as I rode the last three days to Tarifa. But I was lucky. I was very lucky.

The solution to avoid this is simple. Stop and sleep. The first and best prevention is to not reach these levels of sleep deprivation in the first place. When you feel really tired, sleep enough hours to recover. We're all different, but three hours is usually not sustainable for too many days. Some people may even need six hours to compensate for the extreme physical stress they impose on their body for endless hours.

And if you reach this level of sleep deprivation, as soon as you feel sleepy, stop and sleep 10 to 15 minutes. It may seem like nothing, like a 10-minute sleep could not possibly allow you to regenerate your body. But 10 minutes of sleep can make a world of difference. It won't be enough to regenerate your muscle fatigue. It won't be enough to remove any of your general sleep-deprivation state. It may, however, allow you to be lucid for another one or two hours, during which you may continue to ride until you find a proper place to sleep. And in the worst cases, you may even be able to extend your riding with more 10-minute power naps every couple of hours until you find that good sleeping spot.

But 10-minute power naps are not a permanent solution that can keep you going on forever. It's an excellent survival solution. Yet when you're riding your bike at this level of sleep exhaustion, you usually have no power at all, and you are thus not efficient in moving forward. You'd waste less time by getting a proper few hours of sleep and riding effortlessly and faster thereafter. Sleep management is one of the most important skills ultra-cyclists need to master, for sleep exhaustion may very well be the most dangerous of all conditions they are guaranteed to face. Extreme sleep deprivation is often characterized by sensation of irrepressible sleepiness, hallucinations and stumbling, and slower reaction times. All potentially dangerous while cycling or even trekking in the mountains.

You need to sleep for your body to heal and recover. Sleeping takes time, a luxury that ultra-endurance racers do not have. A power nap is the athlete's best friend. It doesn't require much time. In fact, it's important not to sleep too long.

Power naps

A 2015 study in the *Journal of Sports Sciences* looked at participants in the UTMB (Ultra-Trail du Mont-Blanc), during which ultra-runners run all the way around Mont-Blanc. The time limit is around 46 hours, but the fastest cover the distance in around 20 hours.

Most racers can last 24 hours without sleep. But the benefit of a power nap is so important that many elite racers who plan on finishing within 24 hours take the time to stop for one or two. Racers feel that the boost of energy they gain from a power nap more than compensates for the time spent catching up. Sometimes even as little as five minutes of sleep helps. In this 2015 study, most of those racing more than 36 hours benefited greatly from using power naps.

Sleeping is divided into cycles that last approximately 90 minutes each. Although some online sources simplify this to three main sleep stages (and past research has indicated five stages), a full sleep cycle is now defined by four stages, as outlined by the American Academy of Sleep Medicine (AASM) in 2007.

The first stage is when you start drifting into sleep. This can last 5 to 10 minutes. As your brain slows down, your heartbeat, eye movements, and breathing slow down with it. It's very light sleep that is easy to wake up from.

Stage 2 is when you become less aware of your surroundings and your body temperature drops. Eye movements stop, and breathing and heart rate become more regular as your body prepares to enter deep sleep. This stage can last from 10 to 25 minutes. It reduces fatigue, heightens alertness, and improves mood and performance.

Stage 3 is when your body enters deep sleep. Muscles are completely relaxed, blood pressure drops, and breathing slows. This stage is critical to bodily recovery and growth. Your body regrows tissues, builds bone and muscle, and strengthens the immune system. It can last 20 to 40 minutes and is generally the longest stage, at least during the first cycle. It's believed that adults spend more than 50% of their sleeping time in this third stage, from which it is harder to wake up.

These three initial stages are called the non-REM sleep stages. The fourth stage is called REM sleep, or REMS (rapid eye movement sleep). Brain activity increases, and it is believed to be the most essential state to improve cognitive functions like memory, learning, and creativity. Although the eyes move rapidly and breathing can increase, all other muscles of the body experience atonia, or temporary paralysis. Dreams can happen at various stages, but it is usually during the REM stage that you dream wildly. REM stages make up 25% of our sleep. They may only appear after 90 minutes and be very short during the first cycle, but later into the night the duration of other stages may decrease and the REM stage increases significantly and can last up to an hour.

After a full sleep cycle, which could last approximately 90 minutes, another one starts, repeating all four stages, and this continues until we wake up.

But if we wake up before the end of Stage 3 or during Stage 4, we will feel groggy and fatigued; sometimes even more tired than before the sleep. It's important to sleep through the full duration of Stages 3 and 4. Nap for 30 to 60 minutes, in other words, and you'll hit the deeper stages of sleep and wake up mid-cycle, which will make it very hard to restart cycling.

Chapter 4

We gain a lot by sleeping through a full cycle (~90 minutes). We feel refreshed. But during exercise, sleeping through a full cycle may require the re-warming of all your muscles (even in warm weather) before you can put real pressure on the pedals.

Power naps aren't reserved for athletes. They can benefit most people in their daily life activities. They are, however, particularly beneficial to athletes, and they are the secret weapons of all ultra-endurance racers.

The secret of a power nap is to sleep through stages 1 and 2, but to wake up before you enter deep sleep. The problem comes from estimating the time of these two first stages. If Stage 1 can last 5 to 10 minutes, and Stage 2 last 10 to 25 minutes, then should you sleep over 20 minutes? Probably not, because sleep-deprived athletes may run through these cycles faster. For most people, 20 minutes is the sweet spot, but to play it safe, athletes may want to limit the power nap to 15 minutes.

This is why, during our race across Europe, we set our alarm for 15 minutes.

Managing sleep is of crucial importance in any ultra-endurance sport. Once we know our bodies and have some experience, it's not complicated. The problem is when we race as a pair—in this case, managing power naps and night sleep becomes very complex.

If you're already falling asleep on the bike, you'll want to have a proper sleep as soon as possible. It was difficult for Yumi and me to race as a pair because our rest requirements were not synchronized. When one of us was falling asleep on the bike, we would immediately stop due to safety. The one who was fighting to stay awake on the bike would usually fall asleep as soon as we lay down. The problem was that the other person, even though also tired and sleep-deprived, might not have been exhausted at the same time, thus required five or more minutes to fall asleep. I remember whenever Yumi needed to stop, she would be asleep the second her head touched the ground. It took less than two seconds. Whereas even sleep-deprived, if I had some energy left on the bike when we stopped, I'd be tossing around for five to seven minutes before falling asleep, or sometimes not sleeping at all before the alarm rang. Sleeping five minutes wasn't enough, but a 15-minute power nap was perfect for Yumi. Two hours later, it'd be my turn to fall asleep on my bike and ask Yumi to stop. Unable to fall asleep in such a small window, and because I already stopped more often for food and water, she'd be desperate to get going, feeling we were wasting precious riding time.

Taking the time to allow us both to get a full 15-minute sleep would have meant stopping 30 to 40 minutes. In addition to eating into our riding time, the first person falling asleep would have over-slept into the beginning of a deep sleep stage.

That was probably the toughest part of racing multi-days as a pair. The same was true for our energy levels. Cyclists all hit moments when they have great energy, and others when each pedal stroke feels heavy, and no amount of effort seems to move you forward. The problem is that these moments don't happen at the same time for both people. The second greatest challenge of racing as a pair was to have to constantly adapt our speed to that of the slower person. And the slower one was never the same person. It depended on our energy levels of the moment. These are just a few of the challenges I'll describe in my book about the race across Europe.

Sleep deprivation

Going against the flow of most other ultra-bikepacking events, I imposed a sleeping rule on the Ultra Bike Pursuit. The rule is simple and essential for the safety of cyclists on this mountain course. People can ride as much as they want, without any stop for the first 24 hours. Many ultra-cyclists often like to skip the first night of sleep. But from day two, participants are imposed a single three-hour stop or two one-and-a-half-hour stops, whichever they prefer. This may help them get a two- or two-and-half-hour sleep, what I consider the bare minimum to not fall asleep on a mountain descent. Of course, participants are encouraged to sleep more, and the longer the course you plan to ride, the more you should sleep.

Pierre, who was aiming to finish the 2300-km course, understood this. He was managing his resting time to perfection, always taking great care of his body, ensuring good nights' sleep and warm conditions. Pierre was driven by impressive mental strength. He could certainly ride longer hours and fight sleep as much as the very best, but often racing smart is more efficient than racing hard.

Yvonnick, even though new to these types of experience, also understood it and sometimes stopped early evening to sleep a few hours when he started to feel sleep deprivation. Sometimes he even stopped very early in the evening, as he did in Thuir. But then, after a few hours, he was able to restart fresh and ride fast.

Some people may think caffeine is the solution. Many endurance athletes take caffeine in various forms, they carry caffeine gels, candies, gum, or pills. But caffeine, though it can help to stay awake and alert a little, is not long-lasting, and ultimately will never be enough to keep you awake once you reach that state of sleep deprivation. Caffeine may momentarily reduce the symptoms of fatigue, but it doesn't help the cognitive functions. Plus, too much caffeine can lead to digestion and stomach issues, and other problems, particularly during long endurance races.

Without diving into all the problems that caffeine can bring when overtaking it, and particularly when it's combined with dehydration and exhaustion, here is a little secret about combining it with power naps. It may seem crazy to take caffeine before your power nap, but it can work well. It takes between 20 and 40 minutes for the caffeine to kick in. Taking it before your power nap would have it kick in when you restart cycling and give you a little boost when you could enjoy it most.

Caffeine isn't for everybody though. As a non-coffee drinker, I tried caffeine pills during my Oman desert crossing when I started to fall asleep on the bike. It didn't help, I had to stop and take a power nap anyway. But then I had a very annoying tingling in my head and extremities for a couple of hours, and it didn't feel good at all. As for everything, it's best to experiment before your big event.

The same goes for high-energy taurine drinks such as Red Bull, Monster, and the like. They give you a short boost. In the end, they won't do much more than you biting your tongue or fingertips. A power nap is the only quick survival solution and a few hours of sleep (at least two full cycles) the only real lasting, efficient solution.

Luckily, both Chris and Yvonnick did not try to push beyond their sleep deprivation limits. And Pierre wasn't suffering from sleep deprivation at all.

Chapter 5

Welcome Back to the Hautes-Pyrénées (September 9)

Shortly after 04:00, Yvonnick's text showed up in my WhatsApp. He was back on his bike for the long stretch down that would take him to the town of St-Girons, heading toward Portet-d'Aspet.

At 06:00 it was Chris' turn to take to the road and start climbing to Lac de Lers and Col d'Agnes.

Pierre waited until 07:20 to resume his descent of Port de Pailhères to the town of Ax-les-Thermes. He was now nearly 100 kilometers and three mountain climbs behind Chris. But he was fully rested, warm, and with dry clothing as he resumed his ride.

When Yvonnick reached Portet-d'Aspet at 08:40, he was back to his neighborhood, less than 50 km from his home as the crow flies. You would think that it's a huge benefit to know every twist and turn and slope of all the climbs to the finish line. I certainly thought so, but when I asked Yvonnick, he replied that it was a double-edged sword. On one hand, you know exactly what to expect, and you don't have to worry about navigation mistakes anymore. On the other hand, you know exactly what to expect, and when you're really tired, being ignorant might be a blessing. For Yvonnick knew well how much climbing he had to do, and how tough some of these climbs were. He even knew the little invisible bumps, and he knew that some of them, though not labeled as a col, deserved respect and required more energy to climb than a simple hill.

Living and training in the mountains, Yvonnick is a skilled descender and found no difficulties in the steep technical descent ending with the Casartelli monument. He quickly climbed the eastern slope of Col de Menté, another Tour de France ascent with a fast but technical descent before heading to the mountain pass of Port de Balès.

Etymology

Col is the most widely used French term for mountain passes, but they can also be called *Port* or *Portet*. *Port*, which means a breach or a pass in the mountains, comes from the Latin word *Porta*, a door. It is a typical Pyrenees term often used for mountain passes that are a door, or border between France and Spain, like the Port de Larrau or Port de Boucharo. The term is also used in Spain (*Puerto*) for the same mountain passes, and curiously Puerto del Pourtalet, which doesn't bear the name Port, but Col du Pourtalet in French. Port d'Envalira marks the mountain border between France and Andorra, even though the top of the pass is located a few kilometers within the borders of Andorra while climbing its northern slope starts in France.

Sometimes *Ports* separate regions within the same country, like the Port de Balès that separates the Hautes-Pyrénées from the Haute-Garonne. Portet-d'Aspet marks the border between Haute-Garonne and Ariège. On Port de Pailhères, even though both sides of the road are located solely within the region of Ariège, the road itself crosses the border into the region of Aude toward its top, before returning to Ariège.

But there are exceptions, and sometimes some *Port* or *Puerto* links two valleys within the same region of the same country, like the Puerto de la Bonaigua, entirely within the Spanish region of Catalonia. Maybe it was called a Port because even though it does not mark the political border with France, it is the last Spanish mountain pass of Catalonia before entering France and thus marks the physical border of the mountain range separating the two countries. Or maybe the origin of its name is a secret buried in history like the one of the Port de Lers, its location in the middle of Ariège being far from any regional or country borders.

Other mountain passes are named *Hourquette*, a Gascon name that comes from *Hurkete* derived from the Latin *Furca* which means a fork. Gascon was the old Occitan language spoken in the southwest of France, a region previously called Gascony that was made famous by Alexandre Dumas' writing of the *Three Musketeers*. *Hourquette* describes a mountain pass with a fork or V-shape viewed from above its crest line. The most famous one among cyclists is the Tour de France climb of Hourquette d'Ancizan.

But don't worry if the etymology of all these mountain passes remains a confusing mystery; regardless of their names, all Pyrenees mountain passes offer superb scenery and great challenge and, in this respect, Port de Balès is king.

Port de Balès

The Port de Balès is a fairly recent addition to the Tour de France. It was only a forest maintenance gravel track until it was first asphalted to be featured in the 2007 race. Already featured five times, it's been a favorite of the TDF and Vuelta ever since and has hosted epic battles. The most famous was when Andy Schleck attacked Alberto Contador one kilometer before the top, dropped his chain, and lost the Tour de France by 20 seconds. Contador was later disqualified, so Schleck didn't lose the Tour after all.

But for Yvonnick, it was not a mythical climb on which he had watched legends of the Tour battle it out. It was his backyard, his training climb; a very familiar climb he could easily ride to and back from home. It was a climb he loved, but love has its highs and lows.

Port de Balès isn't as steep as the short Mur de Péguère, but it climbs for 19 kilometers. With a 6.4% average gradient, you would think it's much easier than Tourmalet, but that does not represent its true difficulty. The first nine kilometers are gentle, and the last ten grueling, with nearly three kilometers averaging over 11%. It's irregular too, with short sections of flat followed by 15% monstrous ramps. Balès is very tough. I find it much harder than Tourmalet.

The first few kilometers cross a superb forest with a variety of trees that change as we gain elevation. You start riding through chestnut trees, giant oaks, and beech that around the 1000-meter line slowly give place to fir trees and Scots pine, and the higher you climb, the fewer the trees. Climbing through this thick forest offers you a palette of constantly changing colors with all the gamut of greens, and the early autumn foliage of yellow, pink, and orange until you reach the last kilometers. Above 1600 meters you still find hook pines that slowly give place to open views of green pastures where the only species of trees still growing are the dwarf willows, too low to obscure your horizon views of the rugged mountain peaks. That's when you discover a world of wild mountains, and pastoral meadows with free-roaming cattle and sheep. You can feel the remoteness that makes this a magical mountain, where time seems to have stopped centuries ago.

But Yvonnick wasn't in the mood to enjoy the views. He was struggling, and the love scale for Balès had plummeted down to zero. As he was struggling on the first 15% ramp, he knew it was only one of many more ramps he would have to climb to marvel at the steep narrow road that plunges into the next valley.

After diving to the other side, he climbed the famous ascent of Col de Peyresourde and took the mandatory checkpoint photo, then put all his clothes on for the descent, only to realize that the itinerary wasn't going down yet. He still had to climb up to the ski area of Peyragudes before descending into the Louron valley. That's one of the drawbacks of knowing a region well and being used to riding things in a specific order. Not bothering to remove his warm clothes for the short 1.2-km climb, Yvonnick reached Peyragudes boiling hot and bathed in sweat. A quick spectacular descent took him to the Génos-Loudenvielle lake before his fifth mountain climb of the day.

I met with him on top of Col d'Azet just before sunset. Talking about Balès, he told me, *"Even though I knew this mountain pass well, it felt much harder than I ever thought. It really was a tough climb. Maybe the toughest so far."*

Yvonnick felt great though and thought that maybe he could still climb Col d'Aspin before calling it a day. But reaching the base of Aspin at 20:45, he found a perfect shelter under a bus stop just as his body demanded some rest. And that's how his time to sleep was determined on the spot. When your body shuts down, fighting fatigue is the worst thing to do.

As Yvonnick was dropping off to sleep, Chris was arriving at the base of Port de Balès. Unlike Yvonnick, though, he had never climbed it and knew nothing about Balès. In the village of Mauléon, he contemplated a banner right across the road to welcome cyclists that said, "Port de Balès – 19 km of Joy."

At the same time, Pierre was knocking on the door of a house with an old hotel sign. The hotel had closed over 30 years ago and it was now just a private house. Pierre asked the owner, who was sitting on her porch, for any other hotel around. The lady invited him to stay for the night.

Staying with locals is a personal choice. Some participants may not seek such opportunities like Chris, who feels that sleeping outside is part of the adventure. In some racing events, accepting invitations is even against the rules, which clearly stipulates "only commercial accommodation available to all" but the Ultra Bike Pursuit isn't a race. It's an adventure. And participants can define their own adventure: for some, meeting and exchanging with locals is part of it. A young cyclist may not have the means to pay for many hotel nights. Meeting locals and being invited in can be a wonderful travel experience.

Pierre seemed to be blessed with providence and generous hosts. But maybe it's because he was just being Pierre, a young man who breathes honesty, simplicity, and the joy of life. I think people sensed it and felt comfortable with him. They were also inspired by his adventure, so he got more invitations to lodge in people's homes than other participants.

Chapter 5

But even more incredibly, the village where Pierre stopped for the night was only six kilometers from the start of Balès, where Chris was standing at that exact time. Pierre, again, had closed a gap of nearly 100 kilometers and three mountain climbs to almost catch up to Chris. Even though Pierre was still the last wagon, participants and dot-watchers alike understood that on the bike, he was a real machine. It was also clear that Pierre knew how to pace himself and was enjoying every moment of every day.

After driving down from Azet, up to Peyresourde, and around the mountain, I met him in the small village of Siradan. All showered up and clean, he was relaxing in his pajamas in the living room of his friendly host. He didn't even look tired.

After talking a few minutes with Pierre, I drove up to the Port de Balès to look for Chris.

Port de Balès is not only known for the challenge of its climb but also for its wild, almost undisturbed landscape, with more free-roaming cattle and grazing sheep than people. And what is true during the day takes a new dimension at night. On my way driving up to meet Chris somewhere on the mountain, I had to stop and push away cows from the road. Some were standing, others sleeping right in the middle of it, and they didn't budge. It took me five minutes of yelling and pushing their butts to fight my way through. I imagine that Chris didn't push the cows out of his way but in the beam of his flashlight had to swerve around these massive lethargic animals that in the night seemed to be from another world. At least there was no risk for him to come at full speed and crash into a cow, something cyclists must be aware of when they descend Pyrenees mountains at night.

Cycling mountains at night was like discovering a new world, a world Chris had entered, where the dim moonlight barely broke through the forest canopy and into the deep ravines. Depending on your fatigue level, it could be a dark world where all the rocks, trees, and gentle animals suddenly transform into the wildest things your mind can imagine. The more tired you are, the wilder the imagination. I played with such a description in the book I'm currently writing about our Europe crossing, which would have you think I was stoned. But that can even happen during daytime on ultra-endurance challenges.

I found Chris grinding at a very slow pace, swerving to try to lower the grade of the climb while adding a little distance. He looked exhausted, but how could he not be? It was 22:25. He had been on his bike for seventeen hours on his fourth day.

He told me, *"On the steepest stretches, I had to walk and push my bike. It didn't make sense for me to spend that much energy and move up slower than if I were walking."*

Yes, it doesn't always make sense to ride. There is no shame in walking your bike to save precious energy, particularly when you're spending over 18 hours on your bike daily over such challenging mountain terrain.

Chris was happy to stop for a brief chat. He still had five kilometers to go to reach the top. Despite his obvious exhaustion, he was in excellent spirits, and with a great smile, said, *"I'll make it to the top and descend to the first village where I'll find a spot to sleep."*

An hour and a half later, around midnight in the mountain village of Bourg-d'Oeil, he found a perfect open barn to lay out his bivvy bag and fall into a coma-like sleep.

Chapter 6

Tourmalet for Dessert (September 10)

Before Chris fell asleep, Yvonnick had already woken up. It was around midnight that he resumed his ride to climb Col d'Aspin.

Although Yvonnick had long ago lost all illusions about riding the full course in less than three days, he still believed that he could and wanted to cross the finish line in less than four full days. He had until 08:00 to do so. The long descent of Col d'Aspin took him to the start/finish town of Bagnères. But he was still far from finishing. From Bagnères, there was still a 105-kilometer loop that took cyclists west to the neighboring Argelès valley, up the Luz Gorge to climb the western slope of the mighty Col du Tourmalet before a final descend of its eastern slope to return back into Bagnères to cross the finish line.

Yvonnick had been very lucky with the weather. Apart from the drizzle on the first day, he had mostly been riding in the sun or under an overcast sky, and never got drenched. This was also partly true for Chris. Pierre, on the other hand, had already been soaked twice by thunderstorms.

It was on top of Col d'Aspin that Yvonnick finally got a taste of Pierre's experience. By the time he reached the bottom, in the village of Sainte-Marie, he was soaked and cold, and stopped to change into some dry clothing and rest. Being cold and wet when you're already physically spent makes you feel even more tired. After a short pause, he resumed his ride. I can imagine how he felt as he rode his bike less than 200 meters from

Chapter 6

the finish line, knowing that he still had to ride over 105 kilometers around to the neighboring valley and still climb Tourmalet from its opposite side.

Chris rolled down the remaining length of the Balès descent at 06:00 and started making his way up the Peyresourde climb.

At 07:00 it was Pierre's time to resume cycling and attack the monster climb of Port de Balès. He loved every moment of it and continued to the iconic Col de Peyresourde and ski area of Peyragudes.

From the top of Peyragudes, the view plunged all the way down to the turquoise water of the Génos-Loudenvielle lake. Right behind and above the lake stood fifteen perfect switchbacks that would take cyclists to the top of Col d'Azet. A few years ago, there weren't any roads over this mountain pass. The road ended a couple of kilometers under the pass at the ski area of Val Louron, which was the location of the mountain finish stage of the 1997 Tour de France. Upon request from the Tour de France organization, the department of Hautes-Pyrénées built the asphalted road from Val Louron to the top of Col d'Azet to link with the town of Saint-Lary on the other side. This recently asphalted col, first featured in the 1999 Tour de France, was an excellent addition to an ever-growing number of cycling mountain passes in the region. Thanks to the Tour de France, new Pyrenees roads get asphalted, and old ones are well maintained.

Azet commands superb views of the lake, the mountain pass and the even more impressive steep switchbacks leading to the mountain finish ski top of Pla-d'Adet, as well as the superb new climb of Col de Portet, one of the highlights of the Hautacam Pursuit scheduled to start the next day, the continuation of the Ultimate Pyrenees Pursuit for Pierre.

At the time Pierre started his climb of Balès, while Chris was on his way up Peyresourde, Yvonnick was arriving in the town of Luz, ready to start his final climb of Tourmalet.

Tourmalet, the so-called Giant of the Pyrenees, is one of the world's most famous climbs. It's the single mountain that has been featured most often in the Tour de France since its first ascent was done in the historical Luchon-Bayonne stage of 1910. Since then to 2020, out of the 100 TDF events, the iconic mountain has been featured no less than 87 times. On top, the huge cycling statue of Octave Lapize, the first cyclist to climb it in the 1910 Tour de France, pays homage to all the cyclists who have climbed this Tour de France landmark and will greet you as you conquer it.

Tourmalet is a very scenic and challenging climb. It has an eastern and western slope, and each side displays an entirely different scenery, as if it were two very distinct mountains. The views to the east extend to La Mongie ski area and all its surrounding peaks. Looking west, it's an impressive plunging view toward the Luz valley and bigger mountains in the distance. Just above Tourmalet is the Pic du Midi Observatory, an astrological center set on top of the tallest mountain around and deemed one of the top eight grand tourist sites of southern France. At an elevation of 2877 meters, the observatory was first built in the late 19th century by carrying each stone and material with donkeys, and mostly on the back of porters. Because of its position, the clarity of the sky and the size of its telescope, it's considered to be one of the world's best observation centers. An impressive cable car now takes visitors to the top, and the setting alone offers superb views.

Tourmalet, the single mountain that has seen the birth and demise of most of the legends of the Tour, is so rich in history that entire books could be written about it. It was the perfect final climb for the Tourmalet Pursuit. Ultra-cyclists would finish their epic adventure on the most legendary mountain of the Tour de France. And what a mountain that is.

From the town of Luz, the western slope climbs 18.5 kilometers up, yielding 1450 m of elevation gain, with an average gradient of 7.9%. It starts with three gentle kilometers, with a gradient that gradually increases to up to Km 7 on a road almost entirely straight. At Km 7, the first switchbacks before the town of Barèges signal that the rest of the climb will never be under 8%. The ramps through and out of the town of Barèges already start to hurt. A short welcome 500 m flat stretch is the last chance to relax the legs and spin lightly. After the Super Barèges ski area parking lot, the narrow valley opens up to magical views of soaring peaks. It's beautiful, daunting, and plain scary as your eyes follow the road up a first set of switchbacks, then another one, and farther in the distance to what seems like a mountain cliff you'd never climb on a bike. That is until, high on that wall of a mountain that looms ahead, you see the sun reflecting on a couple of vehicles that would be otherwise too small to see with bare eyes. When you first set your eyes on this sight, all you can think is, *No Way! That can't possibly be the top! I'm not going to climb this!*

And it is this road that will take you over the next eight kilometers to a mountain that seems to disappear into the sky. If you have fresh legs at this point, it's a grand view you'll marvel at. Even better, a few kilometers farther, when you're on the walls of Tourmalet, is the impressive sighting of the Pic-du-Midi looming above.

But if you're tired. If your legs are heavy. If you're not feeling good. If it's a hot day. All you can think about is turning your bike in the opposite direction to enjoy the fast descent of the 11 kilometers you've already climbed and calling it a day.

Legendary climbs haven't made history by chance. And it is with heavy legs, deadly tired bodies, and all their gear that the ultra-cyclists would have to scale this magical and terrible mountain before crossing the finish line.

There is a point in any endurance sport when you've reached your physical limit. You've exhausted every resource your body could give you. You don't reach that point quickly or suddenly. It takes all levels of many kinds of suffering before you even reach that point. Most human beings will quit long before. Some, as soon as the first signs of pain tingle their bodies. Others will cope with some pain until they feel it to be unbearable. Trained endurance athletes can endure incredible pain for hours, but most people have their breaking point before the body reaches a total exhaustion state.

Ultra-cyclists are a different breed of human beings. Most already had years of training as endurance athletes and experienced these various levels of pain hundreds of times.

Before the start, ultra-cyclists know what pain they will inflict on their bodies. But they also know that stopping isn't an option. They are psychologically ready to go through all these painful stages, with the firm intent of continuing to move forward regardless.

Proper training and body conditioning are one thing, but it's never enough. There comes a point when the body just cannot give any more. This is when the vast majority of athletes quit. And this is when ultra-cyclists dig deep into their mental strength to move forward. It takes an incredible mind to overcome all the pains and survival signs your body sends you, and discard them. Sometimes it feels agonizing for an hour, or two, or three. And if you are not entirely committed to succeeding, you won't. It's just not humanly possible.

But winners don't quit. And most ultra-cyclists not only enjoy the marvelous sport of cycling, but they also thrive on exploring their limits, each time pushing beyond what they even thought they'd be able to accomplish. It's not physical anymore. It's all in the head.

And then, after periods of incredible pain, the magical thing that is the body, driven by an unstoppable mind, gives up. It doesn't give up by shutting down and having you collapse. It gives up sending you pain signals. The pain magically fades away. I know, until you experience this, you'd think that's impossible. But really, the pain fades away. It's not that there is no pain anymore, but your brain has been so overwhelmed with pain signals for so long, that it stops paying attention to them.

Suddenly, without any rest, you feel good again. You've won the battle of the mind over the body. I can't properly describe the euphoric feeling, which may also be helped by the huge amounts of endorphins your body is producing at this stage, but it's an amazing feeling. One that needs to be experienced to comprehend.

Experiencing this state, and overcoming your own physical frailty to push yourself beyond any limits, is one of the joys of ultra-endurance sports. A masochistic joy, some would say. But one that yields the most powerful feeling of accomplishment.

Ultra-cyclists don't seek a podium. The goal is to cross the finish line. All finishers are winners. But that's not even the ultimate goal. The true, ultimate goal for ultra-cyclists is to explore their limits, to overcome their

Chapter 6

pain, and to experience the greatest feeling of joy and freedom. Nothing can make you feel more alive than this.

All the petty problems of life, all the stress from work, everything disappears. It's only you and nature. You feel and fulfill every sense in your body. Your mind, as if it was detached from your body, wanders everywhere like a free spirit. It's not cycling anymore. It's freedom beyond cycling. It's a form of enlightenment.

I'm not sure that Pierre had yet experienced this since beginning the Ultra Bike Pursuit. He never seemed to reach any level of pain, pacing himself to remain in a permanent state of pleasure, resting well overnight. Maybe it would come to him, or maybe he would continue to enjoy every kilometer without any pain. Or maybe he was in a permanent state of enlightenment as he keeps riding every day of the year. Or maybe he's just an alien who doesn't respond to the logic of the human body.

But Yvonnick, who was pushing his physical limits, had certainly gone through these stages more than once in the last four days. And after his midnight departure, Yvonnick experienced some of these pains, discomfort, and deep fatigue at various moments in the night and early morning. I can't imagine in what physical state he started his climb of Tourmalet. But I drove to meet him in the switchbacks eight kilometers from the top, where that view of the looming mountain destroys so many cyclists. Yumi and I waited for him, phones at the ready to take photos.

Yvonnick later told me that when he reached that part of Tourmalet, he did something he had never done before. He talked to himself. He talked to his body. On the grueling 12% slopes after the town of Barèges, he begged his body to grant him one final climb at a good pace to make it to the top and finish.

And when we spotted him on the first set of steep switchbacks of the Super Barèges ski station, he looked amazingly fresh. Signs of deep fatigue appeared around his eyes but faded behind a huge smile that split half his face. He was moving fast. Really fast and with great efficiency. I was in awe of the level of freshness and the speed at which he was scaling Tourmalet after more than 1000 kilometers of mountain climbing and less than 12 hours of sleep in the last four days.

It was clear that Yvonnick had gone beyond all those levels of pain. His mind was the only master commander, and the ship, his body, just followed. He was driven, and he knew that even the toughest eight-kilometer climb could not slow him down. He had already won and finished the Tourmalet Pursuit in his mind.

At 09:45 Yvonnick was sending selfies from the top of the pass, his last climb and checkpoint before racing down to Bagnères where he crossed the finish line at 10:30.

After two incredible marathon days, Yvonnick rode the 1100-km Tourmalet Pursuit in 98h35'. That's 4 days, 2 hours, and 35 minutes, averaging 267 km of mountain climbing with 5330 m of elevation each day. A remarkable accomplishment. And even more astonishing for a cyclist who had never ridden any ultra-bikepacking events before.

The first thing Yvonnick said when he crossed the finish line was, *"For the next time, I know what to do. I'll go home, empty my bags, and make two piles. The things I used, and all the extra clothing I brought that were totally useless. I carried way too much gear, and I felt it. I was so afraid of being cold, I brought a mountain of clothes I didn't even use. Gosh, was I stupid."*

We never feel the weight of the bike when we test it on a local hill with fresh legs. It's after hours of climbing mountains that we realize how foolish it is to be hauling so much in fear and planning for any contingencies. But it's always too late, unless we want to part with possibly expensive pieces of equipment and make the local kids a nice Christmas present months ahead of time. Or, there is always the solution to throw out all the food you've carried for nothing. All those energy bars I never had the heart to throw away in Oman, always thinking that maybe later I'd bonk with no food and would need them, even though I couldn't even fathom chewing even one more. Conflicts, conflicts, conflicts...

But the truth is that we never learn how to pack the perfect gear by reading books or listening to others. It's only with experience that it comes, and still, you may never excel. Packing the perfect gear is an art, one that

Chapter 6

you refine with every bikepacking experience. It's the ultimate compromise of comfort and peace of mind with weight and climbing efficiency.

Shortly after Yvonnick's arrival, Chris was lifting his bike over his head to have passers-by take his photo on top of Col d'Azet.

Pierre enjoyed every bit of the Port de Balès, stopping on the way to take photos and still making some impressive times. He swallowed up Peyresourde and Azet to arrive on top of it around 13:00, two hours behind Chris.

On the loop around Tourmalet, Pierre was gradually reeling Chris in. At 19:00, the two men met in front of the bakery of Luz, at the foot of Tourmalet. After taking a selfie together and eating a quick snack of French bread and pastries, they started the final Tourmalet climb together.

Pierre gently suggested to Chris they ride together. Chris, always enthusiastic, tried to stick with his companion for a third of the climb. But in the steeper switchbacks before the town of Bagnères, Pierre, dancing effortlessly on the pedals, was forcing Chris into the red. Chris checked his power-meter, and he was already pushing 250 watts, struggling to stay with Pierre. You may recall my earlier example of the weight comparison between the two, and the difference of energy it takes to scale that specific climb.

That was way too much, a power he could not possibly sustain in his current physical state after so much riding. He slowed down and saw Pierre quickly disappear ahead of him. Pierre did most of the climb standing on his pedals and never even used his 28-tooth. The grades weren't steep enough. The only time he had used his 28 over the last 1000 kilometers was on the Mur de Péguère.

Pierre was on top before 21:00. He wanted to wait for Chris, who was more than five kilometers down. But a chilly wind swept across the top, and he descended so as to not catch a cold. Pierre crossed the Bagnères finish before 22:00, around the same time Chris arrived on top of Tourmalet.

Chris only had to descend to the finish, but for Pierre, the adventure wasn't over. His quest to finish the Ultimate Pyrenees Pursuit continued, and he would need to be well rested to ride the Hautacam Pursuit section that promised even more climbs and challenge. He slept in a hotel in the town of Bagnères.

Meanwhile, a tired and confused Chris rode his bike less than 200 meters from the finish line, and, not paying attention to directions, continued straight into the town of Bagnères from where he had to turn around and backtrack to the finish line. He crossed it before midnight in 111h11'. That's 4 days, 15 hours, and 11 minutes, riding a daily average of 234 km with 4750 m of elevation.

Yvonnick, who had returned home to shower and rest, had set his alarm to drive back to the finish to welcome and congratulate Pierre and Chris. That's the friendly spirit of these bikepacking events.

All participants know what it means to be a finisher. It takes a great amount of strength and perseverance. It takes overcoming suffering. It deserves the utmost respect, something that faster riders understand. It's a personal accomplishment where you've pushed your physical and mental limits beyond what most people could even imagine. When you're a finisher, you're a winner. And at the age of 61, Chris was a winner. With great satisfaction, he slumbered in the luxurious bed of the three-star hotel hosting our finish line, his first real bed in five days. Well done, Chris. What an impressive accomplishment. It was an astounding achievement by all three ultra-cyclists, who would keep fond memories of their ultra-cycling experience in the Pyrenees.

Chris described the Ultra Bike Pursuit as: *"the very finest climbs and scenery on the best roads."*

If the challenge was over for Yvonnick and Chris, it continued for Pierre, who, with the entire Hautacam Pursuit ahead of him, was facing another 1200 km that would take him to the spectacular and tough climbs of the Basque Country.

Chapter 6

Chapter 7

On to the Hautacam Pursuit (September 11)

September 11, 08:00, was the start of the Hautacam Pursuit[1]. It was the first day for Alex and Guillaume, who were taking their places on the start line in the Pyrenees town of Bagnères.

They had fresh legs, and with the adrenaline of the upcoming start pumping in their blood, they were anxious to begin pedaling. They would start riding an hour behind Pierre, and that alone would most likely motivate them to try to catch the young man.

For Pierre, it was the morning of his sixth day and the adventure was set to continue.

The occidental itinerary is even tougher than the oriental Pyrenees route that Pierre just finished. It has more mountain climbs, 30% more elevation gain, and steeper slopes.

Even though Pierre is an extremely strong cyclist who paced himself to perfection over the first five days and slept long nights to offer his body the time to recuperate, the Tourmalet Pursuit nevertheless gave him the toughest days he had ever done in the saddle, and undoubtedly all these climbs took their toll on his legs. Would he be able to withstand an even harder course without any full rest days?

The Hautacam Pursuit starts and finishes in the heart of the Hautes-Pyrénées, taking cyclists west to the Atlantic coast and back. They will cycle

---
1. Renamed the Basque Pursuit from 2021.

many iconic climbs of the Tour de France such as Soulor, Aubisque, Marie-Blanque, La Pierre-St-Martin, Luz-Ardiden, Tourmalet from the eastern slope, and Col du Portet. Hautacam, one of the most amazing Tour de France mountain finishes of all time, is the final climb. Participants will also discover many off-the-beaten-paths climbs and routes.

When I take customers on more leisurely rides in this region, we dive deep into the colorful culture and excellent cuisine of the Basque Country. But these riders will be attempting to cover the route in as few days as possible, which will allow them only to take in the breathtaking scenery without any time for cultural visits, and even less time to eat in one of the fancy restaurants. At least, they might still be able to enjoy some of the local products they can purchase to eat on the go, like the delicious local cheese or traditional cured ham that inside a fresh crispy baguette make for fabulous sandwiches.

They can also enjoy the famous dessert specialty of Gateau Basque that can be purchased from various specialty stores and *boulangeries* (bakeries). The Gateau Basque is a traditional shortcake filled with custard cream or local black cherry jam. The crust is tender inside, and crunchy to perfection outside. Whether you're a cyclist or not, on any visit of the Basque region, you need to try it. The recipes are century-old, well-guarded family secrets passed on from one generation to the next. This is why no two gateau Basque taste the same, but all are divine and every bite produces an explosion of flavors that overwhelm all your gustatory senses and keep you wanting more than you should eat—unless you're an ultra-cyclist about to spend more calories than you could ever swallow. Another benefit of being an ultra-cyclist is we can eat as many Gateau Basque as we want.

The Basque country offers other surprises. As riders will discover across the whole of the Ultra Bike Pursuit[2], the legendary climbs of the Tour de France are not the hardest. Sometimes small unknown passes or even unnamed climbs can surprise by their beauty as well as their difficulty. Al-

---

2. A reminder here to avoid confusions between the name Ultra Bike Pursuit and Ultimate Pyrenees Pursuit. The Ultra Bike Pursuit is the name that encompasses all events, which include the Tourmalet, Hautacam, and Ultimate Pyrenees Pursuits. The website bears its name: www.ultrabikepursuit.com.

though the famous Tour de France climbs of Mur de Péguère and Port de Balès may have been the toughest climbs of the Tourmalet Pursuit, all participants were astonished by the short and relatively unknown Col de Latrape. The Hautacam Pursuit promises even more unfamiliar routes that will put all participants to the test, and unveil a wild landscape even locals may not know.

The 2020 Hautacam Pursuit offered two separate courses, a 556-km Discovery route to be finished in less than five days, and the grueling 1200-km Hardcore route to be finished in just six days. Pierre, who was riding the Ultimate Pyrenees Pursuit, did not have a choice: he was on the Hardcore loop. Guillaume and Alex were on the start line together, but each riding a different course, Guillaume on the Hardcore loop and Alex the Discovery course. Their itinerary would be the same for the first 150 km. On the Discovery loop, Alex would still discover some of the most scenic and challenging climbs in the Pyrenees, not to say in Europe or in the world.

Most cyclists use distances to qualify and quantify their rides, training races, and events. But in the Pyrenees, distances are meaningless. After all, a strong ultra-cyclist could cover 556 kilometers in a day and 1200 in two, if the roads were perfectly flat.

Mountains change everything. Most mountain events include a few mountain climbs and a lot of flat. That's even true of the Tour de France. But not the Hautacam Pursuit. If the 22,000 meters over 1100 km of the Tourmalet Pursuit that Yvonnick, Chris, and Pierre just finished seemed impossibly hard, it fades in comparison to the 33,000 meters the cyclists will ride over the 1200 km of the Hautacam Pursuit Hardcore loop. To return to the Everest analogy, it's the equivalent of climbing Mount Everest from base camp almost 10 times in six days. It's an unthinkable amount of climbing, even for someone with fresh legs like Guillaume. Even more so for someone who has already ridden the Tourmalet Pursuit like Pierre.

The Discovery route Alex would be riding is shorter, but with 13,400 meters of elevation, it remains a great challenge. Although possible for most cyclists over five full days, the speed or duration determine its difficulty.

And although this route includes almost 20,000 meters less elevation than the Hardcore loop, it nevertheless includes the toughest climb in France. A climb so tough that as the organizer, I decided that it would no longer be mandatory in future events. I will make it optional because the majority of cyclists would not be able to climb it with a loaded bike, even on fresh legs. It's that monstrous of a climb. But for 2020, it wasn't an option you could bail from. You had to ride it or scratch from the event. And for Alex, it would come after 230 kilometers and nearly 5000 meters of climbing. He had to pace himself well. Pierre and Guillaume would face the monster with even more distance and elevation in their legs.

Before the starting bell rings, let me introduce you to Alex and Guillaume. When they lined up at the start, they seemed strikingly different.

Alex Montegut, 39 years old, with black hair and a fairly dark complexion, stands at 1m72 and weighs only 64 kg, the same featherweight as Yvonnick. He is also ripped. The muscles from his thighs are exploding out of his bibs and the sharp cut of his calves would be the envy of most cyclists. With his small stature, light weight, yet impressive muscles, his look screams power, and that's not false advertising for Alex is an explosive climber who loves steep hills.

Standing next to him, a full head above, fair skin, chestnut hair, blue eyes, Guillaume Labedan towers above him at 1m87. He looks much younger than his 36 years. His legs reveal long, well-cut muscles that also scream power. Very light for his tall frame at 74 kg, Guillaume is also a talented climber. But a little heavier than pure climbers, he prefers the long, more regular climbs, and excels equally on the flat roads, making him a versatile all-around cyclist.

Both cyclists live and train year around in the Pyrenees. They know all the mountains, and are both excellent descenders.

It promises to be a good match between these two men, who will cover the first 150 kilometers on the same itinerary before heading in separate directions.

Alex, a native of the Hautes-Pyrénées, started road cycling only four years ago to improve his endurance for ultra-trail running while minimizing traumas often caused by the impact of long-distance running. Initially, the bike for him was just a tool for recovery and to improve his trail running performance. He immediately loved it, but he never rode a lot. He mostly did short outings and took part in a few cyclosportives that he just rode casually as training.

A nature lover, he had started trail running to enjoy the mountains without taking too much time. He quickly became interested in the toughest mountain ultra-trail running events. In 2017, to improve his trail performance and to accompany his wife, he started running on the asphalt and completed a marathon in 2h44'. Before COVID changed his goals, he had planned to participate in the 100-km road championship and aimed to run the marathon in 2h40'.

With COVID and the cancellation of marathons and ultra-running races, he was able to ride a lot more in 2020 and wanted to try his first ultra-bikepacking adventure on the Discovery course.

Like Yvonnick, Alex is a friend of mine. We've known each other for a few years. He had the advantage of knowing not only all the climbs in the Hautes-Pyrénées but also some in the Basque Pyrenees, but he didn't know the toughest of them all.

In addition to endurance, thanks to his experience in ultra-running, he should be well versed in managing effort and sleep, organization, and navigation skills. But muscularly, the efforts between long-distance running and cycling are very different.

Could Alex, with little cycling experience and being a complete novice in ultra-cycling and bikepacking, draw from his ultra-trail running experience to complete this challenge? Would he make the same equipment mistakes Yvonnick did?

When I asked Alex what his time goals were, he replied he didn't know. But I knew Alex to be a very competitive man. And if he didn't want to say exactly how long he might take, he certainly didn't plan on riding the 556-kilometer course in more than three days, for he had only taken three days off work to participate. And he later told me that he planned on riding

Chapter 7

it in less than two days. That's an ambitious undertaking that would force him to ride fast and to stop as little as possible.

Would he start too fast based on his only experience with fast-paced mountain cyclosportives and bonk after his first day? Without the luxury of time, he might not have a choice. The question was, could he sustain a fast pace through the entire event or would he be forced to abandon before the finish line?

Guillaume lives in the Atlantic Pyrenees. He was born in Paris, but his grandparents are from the Pyrenees, a region he loves and moved to only five years ago. That's when he started cycling. He rode a bike more and more regularly and had diversified the disciplines more each year.

Not a competitor, but rather attracted by the challenges and the scenery, he started naturally with the great mountain cyclosportives with varying success and some abandons. He also tested himself riding the cyclosportive (amateur) versions of two of the five Monuments (the great one-day classic cycling races which are the oldest, most prestigious and hardest one-day UCI World tour races), the Tour of Flanders and a Liège-Bastogne-Liège, each time pushing back his kilometer records. With these races, he understood from experience the effects of dehydration, food cravings, and hypothermia.

Member of a racing club in Pau for three years, he only joined them on a few Sunday outings, because he prefers not to rub shoulders at high speed going around in circles. Cold weather and rain do not deter him and he even likes to roll his wheels in the snow at the top of the open passes in the heart of winter. In all seasons, an hour by bike from home, the mountain provides him with a constant change of scenery.

He is still testing several disciplines to discover his tastes in cycling. The previous year, he had crossed the Alps with friends in 36 hours, in relay mode, a magical experience that gave him the desire for adventure and allowed him to start understanding the body's unsuspected resources after such a long period. Since then, he had been eyeing ultra-events with a mixture of apprehension and addictive attraction. Finally, his friend Sylvain, a mutual cycling friend riding with Yvonnick and me, convinced him to embark on the Ultra Bike Pursuit. He prepared well for it, even if he also discovered long-distance discomforts such as neck pain, saddle pain, weight loss… But as he said, *"We'll see how the training pays off."*

Guillaume had an enormous advantage, a Pyrenean at heart, he not only lived near Pau between the start location and the Atlantic coast, but he traveled extensively throughout the entire region, doing a lot of cycling on these mountains. He knew every mountain climb on the route. Not most of them, like Alex, but all of them, including the off-the-beaten-path ascents, and he also believed that he knew every small road from start to finish. But this advantage can backfire. When you know the mountain passes by heart and no longer dread them, you can swallow them at full speed as usual. But in training, no one rides 1200 km with more than 33,000 m of vertical drop, and with luggage.

And then there were still minor roads in the Basque Country that Guillaume had quickly skipped over that he did not know, and they could hold surprises for him. As all three participants on the previous Tourmalet Pursuit had discovered, an elevation profile chart over 1200 kilometers with giant mountains tends to hide what look like nothing but small bumps, insignificant hills, but mere pimples on a map that are just waiting to destroy you.

Although participants had up to six days to complete the challenge, Guillaume, because of work commitments, only had five days. He started with the confidence that he wouldn't need more. Even without any ultra-bikepacking experience, he was confident in his long-distance cycling abilities, and his thorough knowledge of the region. But if he was wrong, if the six-day full duration of the event was required, he would not be able to complete the event. Maybe Guillaume should have taken an extra day off work. Five days was what Chris and Pierre took on a shorter course with 30% less elevation gain. Guillaume would have to ride fast. Maybe too fast to be sustainable for multiple days.

By now, you know Pierre. His relative freshness after his riding of the Tourmalet Pursuit was already an impressive achievement. But I didn't tell you the full story, and before Pierre starts riding on his sixth day of the Ultimate Pyrenees Pursuit, maybe I should shed some more light on this young man and his true quest.

Pierre Charles is not an average young cyclist. He is a passionate ultra-cyclist on a mission. At 28 years old, he is the youngest participant of the Ultra Bike Pursuit, and the only one who took on the Ultimate Pyrenees Pursuit, which includes both the Tourmalet and Hautacam Pursuits back-to-back with no breaks. That's 2300 km on mountain routes with over 55,000 meters elevation gain to cover in less than 12 days. Registering for this event is setting yourself for the challenge of a lifetime, but that was not enough for Pierre.

In early August, Pierre had left his home in Lyon for a bikepacking race across France that started from the town of Cannes, southern France, and finished in northern France. He rode his bike 1500 km to line up at the start. He raced 2600 km with 30,000 m of climbing through the Alps and met his parents at the finish. He placed eighth in a pack of strong ultra-cyclists, including a few international stars. You'd think he was happy to take a lift home with his family, who greeted him at the finish. But he didn't.

He randomly picked an itinerary that would take him over French regions he didn't know, swung by his parents' place to say hello, and without a rest day, he rode another 2500 km to line up to the start of this Ultra Bike Pursuit race.

When we talked, I wasn't sure I understood. It didn't seem possible, so I had to ask him to repeat. Yes, he rode a daily average of 250 km, including a 2600-km race without a single rest day, from early August until he started the Ultra Bike Pursuit on September 6! Before even taking the start of the Ultra Bike Pursuit, he had already done 45,000 kilometers on his bike this year alone. That's more distance than most professional cyclists ever ride in a full year. And that included a two-month COVID confinement during which he couldn't ride.

Before he even began the Ultra Bike Pursuit six days earlier, Pierre's achievement was already outstanding, and so was his overtraining. No matter how mentally and physically strong you are, even the best world athletes need rest days to recover and rebuilt muscle tissues.

Overtraining is a frequent problem high-level endurance and pro athletes experience. When it happens, you lose power, you lose energy, and your body feels desperately tired. Often, the mind follows and you lose all your motivation. It's a long downward spiral.

Pierre lined himself up to the start of the Tourmalet Pursuit already in an extreme overtraining state, which helps explain the long stops he took to rest every night. But even with longer nights, it couldn't be enough for his body to keep functioning at optimal efficiency. He had to be in survival mode, not far from a full-body collapse. Any coach would have urged him to take at least a full week of rest before entering the Ultra Bike Pursuit.

On the eve of the Tourmalet Pursuit, I had asked him if he wasn't tired. He said, "Yes, I'm exhausted. But I can manage it. I know when I can keep pushing and when I need to take an easy day. I keep a fragile balance to stay on the edge and keep riding."

But with already over 7000 km without any rest days, could he really make it to the finish line of the Ultimate Pyrenees Ultra Bike Pursuit? He still had 1200 km of mountain climbing to achieve this feat, and the itinerary may be spectacular, but the repeated climbs take their toll. He said that the Tourmalet Pursuit was the most beautiful and toughest event he had ever done. The Hautacam Pursuit was going to raise that stake even more.

If he crossed the finish line, Pierre would not only be a strong young ultra-cyclist, he would become a legend of the sport.

But how much longer could he push his body in such a state of overtraining? Would Pierre collapse on the succession of mountain climbs even more challenging than the toughest itinerary he had ever ridden in his life?

Chapter 8

Day Six of the Ultimate Pyrenees & Day One of the Hautacam Pursuit (September 11)

September is usually the driest month in the Pyrenees, often blessing cyclists with non-stop sun, and usually the last heatwaves end in August, making September until the first week of October the absolute best time to ride a long ultra-distance mountain event in the Pyrenees.

Thunderstorms may always happen, but they are more common at the end of a very hot July or August day. The Tourmalet Pursuit had started six days earlier with drizzle, Pierre had been drenched in three thunderstorms in five days, and all three participants got a soaking during the fourth night.

All that unusual September weather seemed to be in the past now. The weather forecast called for bright sun for the following few days, and even some hot weather. Over these long distances on such a strenuous event, it meant cyclists would have to pace themselves even more, drink a lot of fluids, and take supplements to replenish their salts to prevent cramping and possibly more serious problems from the heat.

They might also have to protect their skin from sunburn. On long distances, the sun can be an even greater enemy than rain.

As Alex and Guillaume stood on the start line, Pierre had resumed cycling on his sixth day with a 07:00 start, giving him a short one-hour lead on the pair. It was not a big lead over these two fresh-legged cyclists who were eager to race away…

Chapter 8

They not only had the benefit of fresh legs and fully rested bodies. They also knew every climb of the entire itinerary, or almost every climb. In theory, this local knowledge should help them better pace themselves.

They started riding at 08:00 and together climbed up the small, scenic, grueling hills taking them to the Argelès valley. They swallowed the main hill of Croix-Blanche ending with a 16% pitch as if it was flat, which is how it looked on the general profile compared to the surrounding giant mountain climbs. The two new riders seemed equally strong and rode the first hours matching each other on the climbs.

The first major mountain climb was the Col du Soulor, which they ascended from the north. I waited for the cyclists a kilometer before the mountain pass, surrounded by horses grazing peacefully in a landscape that could have been the setting of a Hollywood movie. High mountain peaks crowned the full valley called Cirque du Litor and an impressive road carved directly into the cliff linked Col du Soulor to Col d'Aubisque. It's one of the favorite helicopter views on the Tour de France, a magical cycling route that all cyclists dream about.

From the village of Ferrières, the north slope of Soulor was a 12.1-km climb at an average of 7.6%. Making it up in an hour or less is a feat reserved for the strongest cyclist with fresh legs on ultra-light racing bikes. That's when you finish in the red, in full hypoxia, throw yourself onto the ground below the sign that says "Col du Soulor," lie down for 10 minutes to catch your breath, and then stand up for the souvenir photo that will immortalize your superhuman effort and illustrate all your bragging back home. You then call it a day, not putting any more pressure on the pedals as you zoom down to your comfortable hotel and the guaranteed treat of a well-deserved cold beer. At least, that's the way it is for many cyclists you see on top of such a famous climb, even when they take an hour and a half or longer to the top.

For most strong cyclists, breaking the hour would mean climbing at your FTP (functional threshold power) level or at 100% of your maximum capacity that you can only sustain for an hour before collapsing. A very strong cyclist who could manage the hour riding at his FTP level should ride this climb entirely differently on a long ultra-distance day with multiple mountain climbs. It should be at a maximum of 70% of FTP. This means that without a loaded bike and on fresh legs, ultra-cyclists should aim to climb Soulor in 1h26'.

Ultra-cyclists aren't average cyclists. Nevertheless, a strong ultra-cyclist with a loaded bike pacing himself for an event such as the Hautacam Pursuit should probably not do it faster than 1h30' without taking high risks of not finishing the day.

Imagine my surprise when Pierre made the climb in 1h13'. That was too fast. Way too fast! But Pierre probably didn't know much about performance training, FTP, training zones and overtraining, and he couldn't care less. He always rode his bike on feelings, enjoying every moment of every minute. But training zones are important.

🏔 FTP & Training Zones

You will often hear endurance athletes talking about their training zones. Without diving into technical details, it is interesting to have a general idea of what these are to understand the zone level at which ultra-endurance cyclists should ride their bikes during the full duration of their event. These zones are used in most endurance sports, including cycling, running, swimming, cross-country skiing, and many others.

Most serious endurance athletes use a heart rate monitor. Cyclists have an even handier tool called a power meter. It is a calibrated sensor that can be placed on a bike's crank, wheel hub, or pedals to calculate the power output in watts that a cyclist can generate.

Athletes do an effort test at maximal capacity to estimate the maximum output the athlete is able to generate for a full 60 minutes. Tests may be shorter and use tables to re-calibrate the results to an hour.

I briefly mentioned it before, but this one-hour maximal effort measured with a power meter is called the functional threshold power (FTP), expressed in watts. The result from a heart rate monitor is called heart rate threshold (HRT) and is expressed in heartbeats per minute.

Although the power meter is more precise, both figures serve the same purpose which is to calculate your training zones.

The training zones are divided into seven (some tables only go up to five), based on a percentage of your FTP or HRT.

Your Zone 1 is your Active Recovery zone. It corresponds to less than 55% of your FTP. This is the zone in which you warm up. You're able to talk as easily as if you were not exercising.

Your Zone 2 is called the Endurance zone. It's between 55% and 75% of your FTP, depending on your physical fitness. In theory, this is a zone in which you should be able to ride your bike forever. That's true for endurance athletes on a one-day event. That is not always the case for multi-day ultra-cycling events. Many participants, if they stay in the top range of their Zone 2 all day long, will deplete all their energy levels and will most likely not finish the event. Only the best-trained ultra-cyclists can ride most of their time in Zone 2. Most others should ride most of their time between Zone 1, or at least at the low end of their Zone 2.

Zone 3 (76%–87% FTP) is called the Tempo zone. Ultra-cyclists should only enter these zones on the steepest climbs if they can't manage to climb in Zone 2.

Zone 4 (88%–94% FTP) is referred to as the Sweet Spot.

Zone 5 (95%–105% FTP) is your Lactate Threshold zone, the one you've been testing with the maximum power you can sustain for 60 minutes.

Zone 6 (106%–120% FTP) is your VO2 Max; and Zone 7 (>120% FTP) is your Anaerobic Capacity. Zones 6 and 7 can deplete all your energy extremely rapidly, and experienced ultra-cyclists will avoid ever reaching them during an event. In fact, ultra-athletes should always avoid pushing any farther than their Tempo zone.

It's important to understand the basics of these zones for a simple reason. Ultra-endurance athletes, depending on their physical abilities, should aim to spend most of their time in their Zones 1 and 2. The longer they spend in their Zone 3, the more energy they are using that they will not be able to regain without rest. When athletes spend time in Zone 4 or above, they use exponential levels of energy and oxygen that will require them a much greater amount of time to recover from.

On top of Soulor

For Pierre, it didn't matter how he would feel in two hours, or at the end of the day. This morning was a new day, a new challenge. The sun was bringing the outstanding mountain scenery to life, and his legs were feeling good.

Pierre was ecstatic. He couldn't stop saying, *"This is beautiful. It's marvelous."*

And after I took his photo as he greeted me with a great smile, in a boost of joy he sprinted the last kilometer to the top. I'm not kidding. After over 1100 km of racing, and with another 1200 km to go, he put the hammer down and flew to the top. That was crazy!

In the space of these three minutes, he had probably pushed into his Zone 5 and filled his legs with lactic acid and shot his muscles. I thought Pierre was a master at pacing himself, but I realized that Pierre was just using the bike to express his feelings of the moment. At this moment, he was feeling great, and he expressed it all in his pedals. I worried he might pay for it before the end of the day.

Until the base of the climb, the two Pyrenees natives Alex and Guillaume (Guillaume on his ancestral land is a Pyrenean at heart) matched each other, cruising along at what felt for them like an easy pace, but an easy pace for a single-day ride and an easy pace for a multi-day epic mountain course isn't the same. When you climb with someone who has a similar pace it can be motivating, but it can also be very dangerous as most of the time you'll climb faster than you would have on your own. Would two experienced Pyrenees mountain climbers like Alex and Guillaume fall into this trap?

Less than 10 minutes after Pierre, Alex and Guillaume appeared shoulder to shoulder. The two Pyrenees climbers had matched each other. They still looked composed and relaxed, but when I checked their time, I knew they had committed a grave error. They had climbed Soulor in 1h08'. A big mistake they would certainly pay for later.

Why did they do it so fast? Inexperience? Pierre the rabbit looming ahead? Or just the irresistible drive of not falling behind the other guy?

They were not engaged in a one-day cyclosportive with only a couple of climbs. One of the greatest problems for people who don't have ultra-bikepacking experience is to think that you're climbing at an easy pace because your legs are fresh and that you're not breathing hard. But just because you're not gasping for air and agonizing in your red zone, does not mean you're not overspending energy.

If a one-day cyclosportive can be done entirely between your Zones 2 and 3, the same isn't true of a multi-day ultra-distance challenge. You should aim never to cycle for long above your Zone 1. It's the level at which your cardiac rhythm is low enough that you don't tax any of your glycogen reserves and instead use as much fat as possible for your primary source of energy.

As soon as you enter your endurance Zone 2, you're burning more glycogen and need to resupply your body and muscles frequently with energy. You also produce more toxic wastes that your body needs to evacuate. It may seem ridiculously slow to ride in Zone 1, but that's the only zone that will allow you to sustain an effort for endless hours over a multi-day event with little sleep recovery.

Sometimes it's necessary to enter your Zone 2 and even 3, particularly on steeper climbing sections when you need to put that energy down on the pedals just to progress forward. But experienced ultra-cyclists, apart from Pierre, aim to spend as little time as possible above their Zone 1. This is what Chris so masterfully did with the aid of his power meter.

I don't know Alex and Guillaume's FTPs, but I am certain that even if they were on what seemed to them a comfortable pace allowing them to keep up a conversation, with their loaded bikes, they were for the entire duration of the climb at least in the high range of their Zone 2, if not in their Zone 3.

The end of the day would tell whether they pushed too hard on this very first climb. After all, maybe they were like Contador, Froome, and Bernal, freaks of nature with an FTP of over 400 watts, able to climb Soulor in less than 30 minutes, and for them, even with loaded bikes, climbing it in 1h08 took the lowest level of their Zone 1. Maybe they did the entire climb with a heart rate they kept below 90 bpm. I doubt it.

I wondered whether Alex and Guillaume were trying to catch up with Pierre. I didn't think so. The two men hadn't met Pierre, but they had followed him and encouraged him for his first five days, and had the greatest respect for the young man and what he was trying to accomplish. There was no real competition between any of the participants, just a tremendous amount of appreciation.

Pierre, at least, didn't feel the least pressured by the pair riding behind him and reeling him in. He wasn't a dot-watcher, not even of the events he participated in. He never even bothered looking at the online satellite map tracking to see where others were. He had never done so in the last five days. He was riding day after day following his rhythm and feelings. And between Soulor and Aubisque, that meant stopping numerous times to take photos.

Although I thought they would, the pair didn't catch Pierre before Aubisque. Not even in the descent, even though Pierre, who doesn't live in the mountains, is a more cautious descender. It was when he stopped in the village of Laruns to re-supply in a supermarket that Alex and Guillaume took the lead without seeing him.

The next climb, Col de Marie-Blanque, took them over the stunning Plateau de Benou before reaching the wooded top of the pass and diving on a steep straight road they would have to climb on the way back. It was at the bottom of that descent, after riding 148 km, that their routes split.

Guillaume on the Hardcore loop would take a left turn to ascend some of the Asque valley climbs, while Alex on the Discovery loop had more gentle hills taking him straight to the town of Saint-Jean-Pied-de-Port at the base of the monster climb he would probably not tackle until the next day on fresher legs.

Pierre crested the top of Marie-Blanque only 15 minutes behind the pair. He matched their pace. We remember him stopping for long nights and making extremely good times during the day on his bike, always closing a nearly 100-kilometer gap on Chris every day. It's incredible that after 148 kilometers, all three men were still within 15 minutes of each other.

All three were about to enter the spectacular region of the Basque country, one of the wildest and most remote regions of the Pyrenees, where picturesque villages and Basque culture aren't the only local specialties. Ridiculously steep and beautiful climbs were equally typical of the region.

Alexander Dumas and the Musketeers

The cyclists now enter the world of Alexander Dumas, where 400 years ago, d'Artagnan and the Three Musketeers rode their horses on these lands. Even if the historical bestselling novel is mostly the fruit of the author's imagination, the people who inspired his books existed. They were not only real musketeers, but most were born in the Pyrenees region of Béarn that our cyclists are discovering.

Apart from the three years he served King Louis XIII as a musketeer, Athos (or Armand de Sillègue d'Athos d'Autebielle by his real name) lived most of his life in Athos-Aspis, a small village on the banks of the Oloron River next to Sauveterre-en-Béarn, not far from St-Jean-Pied-de-Port.

Henri d'Aramits, known as Aramis in Dumas' novel, was from the town of Aramits, adjacent to Lanne-en-Barétous. He served the king for six years as a musketeer before returning to his Barétous valley.

Isaac de Portau, known as Porthos in the novel, was born in the town of Pau, capital of the Pyrénées-Atlantiques, but he spent most of his life residing at the chateau that he erected in Lanne-en-Barétous. Today known as Château de Porthos, it has been converted into a *gîte,* where you can spend the night. Cyclists will ride right past the castle actually built by

Porthos and can stop there for the night. Imagine sleeping in Porthos' bedroom at the foot of the Pierre St-Martin climb.

Charles de Batz de Castelmore, also known as d'Artagnan, was not a Pyrenees native. He was born at the Château de Castelmore in Lupiac, a short distance north of Pau in the region of Gers, previously known as Gascony.

Finally, Jean-Armand du Peyrer, known in the novel as the Comte de Tréville, was born in Trois-Villes. He was the captain of the musketeers protecting Louis XIII and enlisted his cousins, Athos and Aramis. After retiring, he returned to erect a castle in Trois-Villes next to Tardets at the foot of the Port de Larrau climb.

Apart from larger villages and a few vehicles, not much has changed in these valleys since those days. The main economy remains agriculture and most importantly the production of *fromage de brebis* (sheep's cheese). Shepherds continue to take their sheep to the highest mountains and produce a traditional cheese now protected under the label Ossau-Iraty. Only cheese produced between Ossau valley (base of the Aubisque and Marie-Blanque climbs) and Iraty (Col de Bagarguy) just above the village of Larrau can receive this recognized label. It has won most national competitions and prizes and is often considered one of the best in France, which means one of the best cheeses in the world. Cyclists will meet the hundreds of free-roaming sheep on the top of mountain passes, and get a chance to sample the delicious cheese in all local restaurants, cafés, and markets.

Saint-Jean-Pied-de-Port

I met Alex shortly after he flew in front of Porthos' castle and entered the medieval Basque town of Saint-Jean-Pied-de-Port, the most popular tourist destination inland from the coastal resorts.

A fortified community that mixes the charm of an old stone medieval town and the deep red and green shutters and roofs of a typical Basque village, Saint-Jean-Pied-de-Port has existed since antiquity. In the 12th century, its medieval castle was the property of the kings of Navarre. In the 17th century, the village was further fortified with thick stone walls by the famous architect Vauban. It is after entering through one of its giant stone doors that the village reveals all its charm of cobblestone paved streets and traditional stores.

It's also a famous pilgrimage destination, and is unique as the hub where the three Saint James Ways converge. It's the most popular place for pilgrims and trekkers alike to start their walk on the "French Way" to Santiago de Compostela. This makes it a very lively village, with specialty souvenirs and delicious food shops. It's also filled with auberges and restaurants, where hikers and tourists exchange experiences as they prepare to trek the highlight of the Camino over the Pyrenees mountains into Spain.

This town marked Km 200 for Alex, and it is also the base of what is probably France's toughest climb, which remains unknown to most cyclists as it has yet to be featured in the Tour de France and is too tough of a climb for any tour operator to offer it to their customers.

Arnostéguy-Arthé, the killer loop

There are six ways to climb Col d'Arnostéguy. All are challenging and participants will tackle the toughest. I've never taken anybody up the northern climb featured on the Ultra Bike Pursuit. I enjoy riding it myself, but only when I have good, fresh legs. Taking customers on it would be a guaranteed way never to see them return on any tour. Many would have to walk, and those able to climb it on their bikes may destroy their legs for the rest of their tour. There is a limit most cyclists have between the pain and hardship they are willing to endure to climb a mountain, the beauty it reveals, and the satisfaction it provides.

This northern slope may be the most spectacular, but it is not for everybody. I've never even seen any local cyclists on it. It's a special treat for the Ultra Bike Pursuit participants. But will they still be able to enjoy the scenery, or just want to kill me for every meter of suffering I have planned for them with Arnostéguy?

Alex still looked fresh as he prepared to attack the monster climb of Arnostéguy. This was the only climb of the entire course he didn't know, and by far the most difficult.

Words can't properly describe this climb. It follows the Saint James Way on the most scenic and toughest section of the entire pilgrimage route. As you rise higher on this road, you feel you are entering another world. The green mountains of the Basque country grab you and overwhelm all your senses. The higher you climb, and you do climb high on steep slopes, the more the landscape opens with plunging cliffs, 360-degree views of green rolling mountains, and more free-roaming sheep and horses than you have ever seen. It looks like paradise, but to reach it, you have to pay your dues. The climb is irregular, constantly going up and down, with pitches at over 20%. The average grade is meaningless on this climb.

The best way to sum up this climb would be to take a full Mur de Péguère climb and insert it inside a climb that is a full 15 kilometers. If the average gradient is less than 7%, don't let this fool you; it includes descents and flat sections followed by very steep ramps. It truly is a monster of a climb, but it also yields fabulous views. That is if you're still in the mood to enjoy them. Even a car will sometimes choke on first gear on this climb.

Alex started from St-Jean-Pied-de-Port just before 20:00, with very little daylight left. Right outside of town, the first ramp gives you a good introduction to what's coming. You have to push hard on the pedals just to get over it, with the fear that this grade will continue, and the road suddenly descends and returns with a gradual climb. Enjoy this breather and spin your legs lightly, because you're going to need all the energy you have to make it up the next successions of ramps.

The road was too narrow for me to stay driving close to Alex. I passed him and waited for him three or four kilometers up.

Pierre later recalled seeing his GPS, for a few seconds at least, indicating 29% on this section. On such steep climbs, your speed is so slow that GPS accuracy is very random. Some GPS even enter the pause function, calculating that you're not moving. But at this point, whether it's 25% or 30%

doesn't make much of a difference. It's beyond what most cyclists are able to scale on their bikes.

After 200 km of mountain climbing, even though Alex is a strong climber who likes steep hills, I wasn't sure that with his loaded bike he would be able to climb it entirely without having to get off and push. He rode the entire climb without walking, and although he looked tired and stopped a few times to rest and enjoy the views, he kept a constant smile on his face.

The sunset was turning the mountains into a technicolor palette and all the surrounding hills gradually into a full gamut of greens before darkening into black while the sky inversely started with a pastel pink and moved to dark burgundy reds. As the sun entirely disappeared behind the mountains, it left the dark silhouette of the mountain contours dancing into a sky where the first stars started to sparkle. It looked amazing, and Alex's senses were a mixture of pure pain from the grueling climb after 200 km and the spectacle of nature at its best.

This pain you feel here is meaningful, as it's the price to pay for an epic physical and visual experience that I caught with a couple of short video clips that Alex will remember for years to come[1]. Where most people would have waited for the next day to climb Arnostéguy on fresher legs, Alex, on his mission to finish the next day, wanted to do the climb on day one. If he had waited to do this loop tomorrow, he'd never be able to cross the finish line in two days. But that was an incredible day with a tough final climb to finish with. Would he pay for it tomorrow? Probably…

Guillaume and Pierre, on their longer course, would also face the impressive Arnostéguy climb in a day or two.

The Hardcore loop on this Basque Pursuit included a total of 24 climbs, 11 of which were also included in the Discovery Loop.

From Bagnères, all cyclists started with the combination of Col du Soulor and Aubisque, followed by the southern slope of Col de Marie-Blanque. After the descent of Marie-Blanque, Alex's Discovery route took

---
1. View the short video clips on the 2020 blog: www.ultrabikepursuit.com/blog

him directly to Saint-Jean-Pied-de-Port via the low elevation Col d'Osquich.

Guillaume and Pierre would tackle the three challenging climbs of Col de Labays, Issarbe (Col de la Hourcère), and the southern side of Iraty. They would then ride west on many more hills to reach the Atlantic Ocean before heading back east. They would cover a total of 455 km before reaching St-Jean-Pied-de-Port for the first time. That's 255 kilometers more than Alex that Pierre and Guillaume would have to ride before climbing the Arnostéguy loop Alex just did. After Col d'Arnostéguy, they would also climb Col d'Arthé (not included in the shorter loop Alex was riding) before descending back to the medieval town.

Then from St-Jean-Pied-de-Port, all three cyclists would be back on the same course that returned to the mountain passes of Col d'Aubisque and Soulor to re-enter the region of the Hautes-Pyrénées. For them all, that route section would feature Col de Burdinkurutcheta, the easier northern side of Iraty, Port de Larrau, Col de la Pierre-St-Martin, Col d'Ichère, Col de Marie-Blanque. And after the western slopes of Aubisque and Soulor, Alex's final climb would be Hautacam. But Guillaume and Pierre would have many more climbs before reaching the base of Hautacam.

So as Alex was sleeping with the pilgrims before heading back east toward the finish town of Bagnères, Guillaume and Pierre were still riding west toward the Atlantic Ocean.

Guillaume raced through his first day as if he were on a one-day speed record quest. After climbing Soulor, Aubisque, and Marie-Blanque, instead of continuing with Alex he took the left turn to climb Col de Labays from the Aspe Valley. It's a very little-known road that leads to the famous Tour de France climb of La Pierre St-Martin, and it hurts the legs. Then a fast descent on the glassy smooth road of La Pierre St-Martin took him to the climb of the Col de la Hourcère that crosses the ski area of Issarbe. It's a superb small mountain route that was only known to local cyclists until now, and on which I enjoyed guiding for 15 years. But the secret is out, as it was featured for the very first time in the 2020 Tour de France.

Chapter 8

Issarbe isn't the toughest of climbs, but it's challenging enough. And there, Guillaume started to feel it. He cramped. He probably planned to ride more than 230 km on day one, something he needed to do to complete the course in five days. But with cramps, he stopped early at 21:40 to get a few hours of sleep. With the heat of the day, he was certainly paying for his fast climb of Soulor, and Marie-Blanque.

I think that Alex and Guillaume, who didn't know each other before the start, had very much enjoyed each other's company. They felt their speed matched, but both certainly rode much faster than if they had been on their own, and Guillaume ended up paying for it before the end of the day. Could he recover from his cramps and tired legs to ride even harder every day until the end and finish?

Pierre, who kept up his ultra-endurance pace, enjoyed every bit of the itinerary. He kept sending me photos and texts with words like *"Magnifique."*

For the first time, after a warm day, he decided to sleep outside and ended his ride a mere six kilometers from where Guillaume slept. But Pierre, who planned to sleep in hotels every time the weather was wet or cold, had not taken any bivvy bag, usually an essential piece of kit for any ultra-bikepacker. He relied on his warm change of clothing and a single survival blanket. Woken by the cold, he discovered a big tear in his survival blanket. There was no way for him to wrap himself into it without feeling the cold air. He spent a miserable, freezing night and didn't sleep much. Could this single mistake destroy his chance of making it to the finish in 12 days after what had been 7 days of perfect pacing covering 1680 km out of his 2300-km Ultra Bike Pursuit?

This was an epic day for Alex, Guillaume, and Pierre, each on their own adventure and challenge. But after today's mishaps, could they still succeed?

Chapter 9

Race to the Atlantic
(September 12)

Alex started the morning with heavy legs. A very normal feeling after riding over 260 km that ended with the toughest climb in France. He probably regretted his speedy climb of Soulor. But for Alex, this feeling of heavy legs while climbing was new. He was used to dancing on the pedals and racing his way up the steepest climbs, and not struggling to keep a speed of less than 10 km/h on the Basque climbs.

Of course, the Basque climbs are not just any climbs. They are rugged and steep. The combination of Col de Burdinkurutcheta, Port de Larrau, and La Pierre St-Martin from the tough Ste-Engrâce side alone would be feared by Tour de France pro cyclists. But if Alex was to accomplish what he set out to do, to cross the finish line of the Hautacam Pursuit Discovery loop in less than two days (instead of five allowed), these three climbs would only be his hors d'oeuvre. He still had to ride Marie-Blanque, Col d'Aubisque, and, last but not least, the legendary Tour de France mountain finish of Hautacam. A feat not many cyclists could do in a day, especially with heavy legs and a bike loaded with bikepacking gear.

Luckily, Alex didn't make the usual beginner mistake and started with a bike weighing a total of 12.5 kg. (That's 4.5 kg lighter than Yvonnick's bike and the two men are of similar size and weight.) That's where the experience of ultra-trail running came in. Alex preferred to risk being cold rather than carry too much gear. This had always been his choice on high-elevation mountain trails, and it was his choice for his first ultra-bike event. Of course, it was an easier choice over a distance he planned to accomplish with no more than one night. It would have been harder on the distance Guillaume and Pierre were doing. It was a gamble, but would that be enough for him to cross the finish line today?

I slept on top of the Burdinkurutcheta climb, where I met Alex just before sunrise. He described his legs to be heavy, but he was enthused by the spectacular scenery of the mountains that slowly started to take shape from the receding night. Like most new ultra-bikepackers, Alex was discovering that the sunset and sunrises were the best times to ride a bike. He then arrived on top of Iraty, a few kilometers farther, to a grand view of the sun rising over the Larrau valley, a magical sight of mountain peaks breaking through the rays of the morning sun. After the steep and technical descent with plunging cliffs that took him to the mountain village of Larrau, he climbed up the Port de Larrau and suffered. He was paying for his efforts from the previous day.

I didn't see Guillaume, who had resumed his ride before midnight and had already climbed Iraty from the other side early in the night. I waited for Pierre to follow in his wake. Pierre climbed the superb and grueling Iraty Col in the early morning, standing almost all the way. His style reminded me of fixed-gear riders fighting the steepest slopes with a gear too hard for most to push, rocking the bike from side to side. But despite his loaded bike and the 12% average gradient where I stood, he did so with disconcerting ease. I asked him how he was doing, and as usual, with a giant smile splitting his face, he replied, *"Great, I love this climb. But I'm using the 28 today."* Thank you, Pierre, for your contagious joy of life and inspirational attitude. Pierre was at Km 1350 of his 2300-km Ultimate Pyrenees Ultra Bike Pursuit. A cold, sleepless night wasn't enough to deter him from his mission.

I caught up to Alex on his climb of La Pierre Saint-Martin and his speed had slowed down to a crawl. The climbing star was riding like an out-of-shape beginner who for the first time in his life had attempted a climb way over his abilities. I felt for him, but he kept going. Happy to reach the top, he felt disconcerted to be climbing at sometimes less than 7 km/h, half his normal speed. It was already midday and his wife kept sending messages to ask his arrival time so she could come with their daughters to greet him on Aubisque and later on the finish line. He kept pushing his arrival time back with each reply. With over 100 kilometers and three more major climbs to do when your legs are heavy and all you can think of is rest, it's hard to estimate or even imagine when you will reach the finish. Would he even be able to cross the finish line that night? I couldn't imagine what must have gone through his head as La Pierre Saint-Martin, like an unattainable giant, still loomed ahead, never appearing closer in spite of his endless, slow, and heavy pedal strokes.

Guillaume, after a short but good sleep, raced into the night to reach the Atlantic coast in a very impressive time. There, in the small picturesque harbor town of St-Jean-de-Luz, he took a break to enjoy a much-needed breakfast.

Saint-Jean-de-Luz, an historical taste

There is much to visit, taste, and experience in St-Jean-de-Luz. In addition to the house that hosted the Great King, this typical town is packed with boutiques, including Maison Adam, a cake shop founded in 1660 that has been a well-recognized institution for centuries.

The young baker named Adam, who, at the time, didn't own a shop, offered *macarons* of his invention to the French queen (Anne of Austria, born in Spain, became the queen of France after marrying Louis XIII and then the mother of the Sun King). The almond-paste-based cookies melt into the mouth with an addictive sweet flavor. The queen wasn't there by accident: in order to end long periods of war between France and Spain, she had married off her son, the young King Louis XIV, to the infanta of Spain, the princess Maria Theresa, and she had found a middle ground for the ceremony. So it was not in Paris but in Saint-Jean-de-Luz, at the

Saint-Jean-Baptiste Church, that one of the most important royal weddings in history was celebrated on June 9, 1660.

The queen offered the *macarons* to the young king and his new bride, and the rest is history. So fond of the *macarons* were they that they had some brought to Paris. The new Maison Adam outlived the king.

The young baker didn't invent *macarons*, however. Catherine de Médicis—an Italian noble born in Florence who married King Henry II in 1547 to become queen of France and the mother of three kings whom she strongly influenced throughout their reigns—was already fond of *macarons*. She had some specially made for the wedding of the duc de Joyeuse, the admiral of France, and a *mignon* (intimate friend) of her son King Henry III. This small crispy macaron, named Joyeuse after the town the duke was from, has also lived throughout history. Don't miss tasting a few if you ever cycle in Ardèche (the region northwest of Provence), another wonderful cycling destination. But Mr. Adam's version is the one that melted the Sun King.

The traditional recipe of these almond *macarons* is a preciously kept secret and only handed down from parents to children. Today, the 10th Adam generation will offer you the same *macarons* so enjoyed by the Sun King and his queen. You may know the modern *macarons* that later exploded into a multitude of colors and aromas around Paris. You may have even waited in long lines to get a chance to eat a few and compose your own assortments into a palette of confection at Maison Ladurée on the Champs Elysées, but the only place to find the original ones made for the Sun King are in Saint-Jean-de-Luz or in the second Maison Adam shop in Biarritz. Sampling them, you'll feel like a king or queen.

Back inland toward Saint-Jean-Pied-de-Port

Well-fed, Guillaume resumed his ride toward St-Jean-Pied-de-Port. He knew the mountains Alex had climbed the night before, and he was physically and psychologically ready to attack the Arnostéguy climb, which, for him, on the Hardcore course, would be followed by the tough Arthé climb.

He knew the region and he never thought there'd be any difficulties before reaching St-Jean-Pied-de-Port.

But Guillaume made a mistake, because he knew all the major climbs and the region well and had set out on this challenge without a GPS, because he didn't have one. He had memorized most of the course, but he quickly realized that he could not constantly look at the itinerary on his phone without draining its battery. And that's where the complications started. I had planned this route to take people on the most scenic, traffic-free rural roads. Guillaume didn't know some of these small roads and lost his way. Not once, but numerous times, each time having to backtrack and losing at least an hour. He also didn't expect that a small, unnamed climb would take its toll. By the time he reached Saint-Jean-Pied-de-Port to attack the monster combination climbs of Arnostéguy and Arthé, he was already spent.

I met him at Km 467 in Saint-Jean-Pied-de-Port just after 16:00 as he was going to town to reserve a hotel for his return from the tough loop ahead.

He said, *"I very much underestimated the difficulties of this itinerary. I love it, but I'll never be able to do it in five days. I need the full six days, but I can't. I got to work. I think I won't be able to finish it."*

I could sense his disappointment and fatigue. He continued. *"I should have started with the Discovery loop like Alex. It was foolish of me, without ultra-bikepacking experience, to attempt the Hardcore loop. But I always pick the greatest challenge. I'll do my best and will go as far as I can within my five-day time constraint."*

As I followed him on the steep slopes of Arnostéguy, his fatigue was making me cringe as much as his squeaky bike crank under the pressure on the pedals to grind it up, but like Alex the night before, and like Pierre in the morning, he was still smiling.

Ultra-endurance athletes are a special bunch of outstanding and inspiring people. Even when it gets tough, *abandon* is not a word they understand. How much of the 1200 km and 24 major climbs would Guillaume be able to achieve in five days?

I left Guillaume before he reached the top. He continued into the night to finish this loop and rest in St-Jean-Pied-de-Port, covering 512 km in two days.

Alex didn't stop. He rode through the heavy legs and pain, and after swallowing up the Marie-Blanque climb, he was still pushing his way up, nearly reaching the top of Aubisque. It was clear that no pain would prevent him from reaching the finish before dawn the next day. He was determined to finish during the night, and I had to quickly drive a few hours to reach the finish line to greet him.

I met him again as he was climbing the final and mighty Hautacam in total darkness, with only a portion of the road lit by the powerful but narrow ray of his light.

Mighty Hautacam

I personally have a love-hate relationship with Hautacam. This climb is so familiar to me, and it may count as one of my favorite climbs, both for all the joy and great feelings I've sometimes had on it, and for all the pain and suffering it has caused me. It all depends on your legs and how you feel. On a great day with fresh legs, Hautacam is a gem; on a bad day with heavy legs, it's horrible.

One of the most famous mountain finishes of the Tour de France, this is where many of the climbing legends have made history, including Indurain, Pantani, Amstrong, and one of the last winners to date, Nibali. The climb is made of irregular steps from very gradual slopes to over 15% pitches. This irregularity makes it a climb that pure climbers usually love, whereas heavier built cyclists like me prefer more constant grades on which we can enter to a rhythm from bottom to top. Although there are other more off-the-beaten-path climbs that I prefer, Hautacam and Aubisque are probably my favorites among the famous Tour de France mountain climbs.

Hautacam is also my favorite winter climb. As the road leads to a small family ski area, it is cleared of snow daily. Because there are no trees, and the entire climb is exposed to the sun, even with high snowbanks on a sunny winter day, the road is perfectly dry. On a weekday it's the quietest ski area, almost no vehicles ever climb it, making it a winter climbing paradise. The higher you climb, the better the view over the Argelès valley and its surrounding mountains. On top, you are greeted with a 360-degree view of mountain peaks. Amazing. I made a three-minute video of Yumi climbing it on a sunny February day, surrounded by snow. It's stunning[1].

In the dark, Alex couldn't see the surrounding mountains. He could only enjoy the night view of Argelès town below, and by then, he might have been suffering too much on Hautacam to enjoy any views at all. The name Hautacam refers to the large parking lot on top of the plateau, the place where most people park their vehicles to enjoy the winter sports. It's the name of the ski area and the place used at the official arrival of the Tour de France because there isn't enough space on top. But the road keeps going up another 1.2 kilometers to Col de Tramassel. And when we say we climb Hautacam, we always climb 1.2 kilometers higher to Tramassel. Still, nobody knows the name Tramassel, so we call it Hautacam.

Alex, at 64 kg, is like Yvonnick and Pierre, light, of small stature, and a pure climber. And he loves Hautacam, a climb that he regularly ascends. His best time to cover the 8.2% 15.5 kilometers with 1200 m of elevation is almost an hour (1h01'). But that night, he was barely halfway up when the first hour passed. Two hours of struggle were needed for him to reach the top. If you think that's slow, that's the time the average weekend warrior would take on a light racing bike on super fresh legs if they started with a 10-kilometer warm-up in the valley. For Alex, it was deadly slow. He did it in survival mode at the end of an incredible two days.

The road to the finish in Bagnères isn't flat, just a few more rolling hills, but by now, every rolling hill felt like climbing Everest to Alex. It would take him nearly two hours after his Hautacam conquest to cross the finish line in the next valley.

Alex crossed the line just before 23:00, setting the first time of this Hautacam Pursuit Discovery course with an impressive 39h54' to cover

---

1. You can watch it on her profile page on the VeloTopo website (velotopo.com).

Chapter 9

556 km with 13,400 m of elevation. It's a huge accomplishment that translates into a daily average[2] of 330 km with 7460 m.

It was more than impressive. Not only had Alex accomplished his goal of finishing in less than 48 hours, he also did it by setting a time that would be extremely hard to break.

The interesting thing is that I knew Alex could easily do the Discovery loop, and I suggested he attempt the Hardcore loop. But Alex wanted to test himself on this new sport before attempting something he wasn't sure he'd be able to finish. Probably a smart move. Now we know what distance Alex is going to do next time and he will certainly not aim to take the full six days to do it.

With Alex's finish, only two ultra-cyclists were left on the course. I had left Guillaume on the slopes of Col d'Arnostéguy after he climbed the steep pitches leading to Col d'Elhursaro.

Guillaume confessed later that his pedals were defective and that sometimes clipping out was difficult. Arthé following the monster climb of Arnostéguy is a tough climb on its own. On one of the steepest switchbacks of Arthé, as he was almost crawling to a stop, trying to keep a pace at over 3 km/h to not tip over, he lost his balance, couldn't unclip, and crashed on his side. He said he had crashed similarly three times on that day, each time unable to unclip. When you have no power left, fatigue blurs your thoughts, and your reaction time slows down so much you couldn't avoid a snail crossing the road. When you're dealing with faulty pedals that only release by twisting your foot inward, it's counter-intuitive when during all your cycling years, you've twisted it outward to release. And exhaustion helping, such a simple task as thinking to twist your foot in the opposite direction can suddenly become an impossible one.

Although he didn't injure himself, this was one of his toughest cycling days ever. Yet, when I asked him, he recalled a day filled with incredible experiences and mentioned that he loved climbing Bagargui in the night.

Just as Arnostéguy would no longer be mandatory but an optional climb from next year, the same would be true of Arthé, which made a loop

---

2. The calculation was made as if he had ridden the pace over a full 48 hours.

with Arnostéguy for the Hardcore route. I love these climbs, for they are so wild and remote, away from everything. They are the essence of cycling in its purest form. But this combination of two climbs was already insanely hard on fresh legs, and it was followed by a very steep and technical descent of Col d'Arthé. When a cyclist as strong as Guillaume reaches such a state of exhaustion to crash three times on this loop, even though he was riding with defective pedals, as an organizer I have to recognize that it's too hard for most ultra-cyclists to ride without taking unnecessary risks. Guillaume had already done these climbs on fresh legs and he loved them. But nobody will ever have fresh legs when they tackle these monsters on the Ultra Bike Pursuit.

Although Guillaume did great on his second day spending 21 long hours on his bike, he understood from mid-afternoon that he wouldn't be able to finish the Hardcore course. If only he had been able to take another day off from work to use the full six authorized days…

Chapter 10

Flying over Mountains
(September 13)

On September 13, his third day, Guillaume set off early and swallowed an impressive number of climbs, all featuring superb and ever-changing mountain scenery, each more challenging than the last. These were climbs feared by pro sprinters and that always guarantee fierce battles in the Tour de France: Col de Burdinkurutcheta, Port de Larrau, La Pierre Saint-Martin. He struggled a little on La Pierre-St-Martin but soon found his legs again as he quickly climbed Col d'Ichère, and the tough western slopes of Marie-Blanque. He then followed with an ascent of Aubisque and Soulor by night, an experience he called a revelation. Like Yvonnick the week before, Guillaume discovered that he loved climbing at night.

Climbing in pitch-dark, you see a beautiful black sky filled with sparkling stars and the contour of mountain shapes. Free-roaming animals pop up on the road from nowhere. Apart from animal sounds the roads are quiet, not a single motorized vehicle breaks your communion with nature. Sunsets and sunrises are the absolute best times to climb mountains. Away from the heat and harsh rays of the sun, the mountains change colors to show their most enchanting sides. The air is crisp, and the experience yields a feeling of freedom you can't experience during the day.

When you climb at night, sometimes visions, hallucinations, and imagination all blur into one, depending on your consciousness level. For Guillaume, it happened on a road between Iraty and Burdin-Olatze, a very

Chapter 10

scenic, narrow, and remote road, and probably the worst maintained of the entire route as well because it isn't on any of the itineraries of the Tour de France. Sometimes, the most remote roads aren't in the best of shape.

As often happens, sheep and cattle were wandering everywhere on the road. He had resumed riding at midnight and had only climbed Iraty so he wasn't tired, yet as he cycled in the dark with his flashlight only highlighting things within its beam, after avoiding a few potholes he had to swerve around white masses that seemed to him like icebergs. Bizarrely, he felt he was no longer riding a bike but piloting a boat slaloming around icebergs in the middle of the night. What he imagined to be icebergs were cows.

On his third day, Guillaume felt great for most of the day. He didn't feel tired; his legs were strong. After an incredible ride that saw him cover 240 km with a total of five major climbs without counting all the smaller ones, he reached the village of Agos-Vidalos and found shelter under the small roof of a bus stop. He finished the day with good legs and in excellent spirits, despite having developed some saddle sores. He regained confidence that maybe he could complete the entire course in the two more days that his work schedule still allowed for. And frankly, after today's performance, there was no doubt that unless he had a mishap, he'd be able to cross the finish line in the next couple of days. It had been an impressive comeback after how miserable he had felt on day two.

Pierre, riding a half-day behind Guillaume, took the time to purchase a small bivvy bag on the coast. Freezing with his survival blanket the previous night was an experience he didn't care to repeat. From the village of Itxassou, he cycled on narrow roads bordered on one side by cliff and the other by the gentle flow of the Nive River. Soon after passing through an arch, he found a small auberge to spend the night, in a place known as Pas-de-Roland. What our valiant Pierre didn't know is that he had stopped at a historical site that saw the death of the valiant knight Roland and the birth of one of France's most enduring legends.

🏰 Roland's legend

Charlemagne, also known as Charles the Great, was king of the Franks from 768, and then later emperor of the Romans from 800. During the early Middle Ages, he united most of western and central Europe. In 778, with a formidable army, he marched through the Pyrenees into Spain, wresting control of the entire peninsula from the Moors. On his way back to Francia, he sacked the Basque town of Pamplona, believing that the Vascons (Basques) were supporting the Arabs and that Pamplona could later be used to prepare offensives against the Franks.

Roland (also known as Orlando or Rolando) was Charlemagne's first and most heroic general and a popular figure. When Charlemagne was on his way back to France, the rear guard of his army, commanded by Roland, was ambushed in the mountains by the Basques in retaliation for the destruction of their capital. His heavy artillery and equipment rendered all his moves cumbersome. Charlemagne's army was overwhelmed by the much smaller Basque army, fighting with lighter weapons and good knowledge of the terrain in what is known as the Battle of Roncevaux Pass. As the king retreated, Roland held the ground with the rear guard to try to stop the Vascons from crossing the border, allowing Charlemagne time to organize his heavy army to fight and repel the Basques in the lower grounds.

It is in these mountains, at a place known today as the Pas de Roland, where Pierre spent the night. It is also where Roland died from his battle injuries.

He didn't die in vain though, as he had ensured the future victory of the Franks. His act of valor and resulting heroic death were sung all over the Frankish territory (most of Europe), until they became the stuff of legends. It is said that they were the origins of the code of honor that all future knights would later live and serve by.

Although Roland is still believed to have been Charlemagne's nephew, history is fuzzy on that point because his story has been a word-of-mouth tale for hundreds of years. As for the rest, the myth has become grander than the man himself.

The 11th-century song "Chanson de Roland" further forged his name into history, telling of the heroism of Roland with his valiant horse named Veillantif and his magical sword, Durandal. Swords were the first weapons invented by men (spears and bows and arrows were originally made for hunting), but in the Middle Ages they became more than weapons; they became the knights' best friends. It was believed that good swords could pass on energy to good knights and vice versa. Knights all named their swords, and some were believed to have magical powers. Among the three most famous were King Arthur's Excalibur, Charlemagne's Joyeuse, and Roland's Durandal. I have recounted here what are believed to be historical facts, but legends often make better stories, and so does the "Chanson de Roland."

In the song, the Vascons, too few to have offered Roland the glorious death he deserved, were replaced with a massive army of well-armed Saracens. The 11th-century legend from Roland's song would have him commanding the rear guard and staying in Spain while Charlemagne, after seven years of Spanish occupation and an agreement with his rival, the Saracen King Marsile, returned to France with the bulk of his army. Following Roland's suggestion, Charlemagne asked his trusted emissary Ganelon to negotiate with Marsile. Furious to be left behind, Ganelon convinced Marsile to attack the rear guard of Charlemagne's army still in Spain and led by Roland. After fierce battles, Roland and his army retreated to find themselves trapped at the foot of the Basque mountains.

Olivier, Roland's friend and second-in-command, begged him to blow his Oliphant horn to call Charlemagne to the rescue. But the brave Roland still believed they could hold their ground on their own. He refused to blow the horn until his army of 20,000 Franks was surrounded by 100,000 Saracens. When he blew the horn, Charlemagne immediately came marching to help his nephew, but he arrived too late.

Powerless to escape from the massive Saracen army, and determined not to let Durandal fall into the enemy's hands, Roland decided to break his magical sword against the side of the mountain. He tried numerous times, cutting a breach into the mountain, known today as the Pas-de-Roland.

Unable to break the sword, in his last effort before dying of exhaustion, Roland prayed to Archangel Michael to guide his sword as he threw it back to France. The magical weapon allegedly traveled 300 kilometers before pitching itself into the rocky cliff of Rocamadour, where it could still be observed until recently. The medieval town of Rocamadour was already a famous pilgrimage site, and for centuries pilgrims and tourists could observe Durandal stuck into the cliff. In 2011, Roland's sword, one of the most famous in history, was removed from the rock to be displayed at the Cluny Medieval Museum in Paris alongside many other famous swords (a must-visit museum for medieval enthusiasts).

Italian Renaissance artists amplified the legend further with two poems[1], which might have been the birth of modern literature.

Roland's legend would be expanded even further by Baroque composer Jean-Baptiste Lully, who wrote the *Roland* opera, first performed at Versailles in 1685 for King Louis XIV.

Over centuries of word-of-mouth, troubadours took liberties with the song's original lyrics, giving rise to a second variant of the legend, which I'll tell you when our valiant cycling knights reach Gavarnie.

A big scare for Pierre after swallowing the killer loop

After his night in the gorges around Pas-de-Roland, Pierre cycled on a beautiful road that snakes its way up following the contour of a river with a rollercoaster-like succession of hills to return to the main road. Arriving in St-Jean-Pied-de-Port, he had to tackle the monster climb combination that Guillaume had done the previous night: Arnostéguy and Arthé.

---

1. *Orlando Innamorato* by Matteo Maria Boiardo and *Orlando Furioso* by Ludovico Ariosto.

Chapter 10

A guaranteed leg killer, even if you ride with a 34-36 gearing, it's masochism if you only use a 32 cassette as Guillaume did; and just plain impossible if you're carrying a loaded bike, don't have fresh legs, and all you have is a 28 cassette to climb these mean and gruesome slopes. That's exactly the cassette Pierre was using. Even for a powerful climber on fresh legs with no bags, climbing Arnostéguy on a 28 would push the limits. But Pierre didn't seem to have any limits, or if he did, he just hadn't found them yet. He also reported experiencing gale-force winds on top.

He commented: *"Even the sheep had a hard time standing up, I was afraid one would fly away and take me out."*

This set of climbs alone would force most riders to put an end to their ride for the day. Many cyclists wouldn't even be able to complete this loop. Pierre climbed it all without ever setting a foot down. He said his cadence slowed to a mere 30 rpm^2. My knees hurt just hearing these words. I've always used a 34 on this climb, and always wished I had more, like a full mountain-bike gearing.

Both Alex and Guillaume called it a day after this climbing set; granted, they had finished it in the night, but they took a rest before moving on to the other Basque ascents. Pierre tackled them in the middle of the day, and then tackled the steep walls of Burdinkuretcheta, the easier slope of Bagargui, and should have called it a day when reaching Larrau. But with the Port de Larrau looming only 12 km above his head, he pushed for yet another climb. After scaling three of the toughest climbs in France in a row, what is another 12 km at an average gradient of 8% with no less than 6 km averaging over 10.5%? This climb alone is more than enough for regular cyclists. For Pierre, it was just dessert. And when he later sent me photos telling me how amazing the climbs were, I knew he hadn't suffered on it. Or if he did, the joy still far surpassed the pain.

On top of Port de Larrau, he wrote: *"Eighth dream day. May this journey never stop!!!"*

That's Pierre. We know him by now. A joyful and humble monster of a climber.

---

2. Rotations per minute.

But joy can come to a sudden stop when things go wrong. And after reaching the top of Port de Larrau, unfortunately, things went wrong for Pierre.

In the descent, the cable of his front brake snapped, and he was left with only the rear brake. Do you remember the slopes? Six kilometers at an average of 10.5%, with ramps sometimes as steep as 15%. Road cyclists know that unlike with the fat tires and disk brakes of a mountain bike, road bikes get 70% of their braking power from the front brake. And squeezing a brake without a pause, something he had no choice but to do with the rear, can overheat the rims and blow a tire. Pierre got scared when his brake gave up, but he descended all the way back to Larrau with his rear brake alone and making good use of the heels of his shoes. Luckily for him, like many ultra-bikepackers, Pierre had opted for mountain bike shoes instead of the more rigid road cycling ones that would probably not have helped to slow down the bike while dragging them on the road surface. In Larrau, he managed to play with the extra length of his cable and fix it with his multi-tool, but exhausted, probably as much by his descent as by his entire 12 hours on the bike, he called it a day and stayed there for the night.

There are worse places to stay than in the picturesque mountain valley of Larrau, where the sunset and sunrises are a MUST experience. To end his day, Pierre sent me this message:

"Small day in terms of kilometers but so strong in emotion, and physically GARGANTUAN, in short, one of my most beautiful 🤙 🤙 🤙."

It was another day filled with accomplishment from our ultra-warriors, who, maybe the following day, would leave the Atlantic Pyrenees behind to re-enter the region of Hautes-Pyrénées.

Chapter 11

All Kinds of Pain
(September 14)

Ultra-cyclists can take pain, a lot of pain. Pushing physical and mental limits is what ultra-cyclists do. All embrace pain as a necessary step to reach revealing and often enlightening moments.

The body is an amazing machine, and the more you punish its muscles, the stronger it becomes. With strong mental will, you can experience the toughest day of your life and be in the best shape the next day. This is how quickly the body of ultra-cyclists can adapt.

I remember in Oman, after the toughest 24 hours I had ever done on a bike. On day one, I rode 401 km with 5000 m of elevation through the desert and on steep dirt road mountain climbs to reach the base of the main ascent. There, I bonked on the monstrous desert mountain climb of Jebel Shams, seriously dehydrated after a full day at almost 40 degree Celsius. I feared my legs would cramp or seize. At best, they would feel very heavy and I'd have no power at all. No night of sleep could possibly be enough to recover. I slept less than four hours, and felt amazingly well. My legs were on fire, so much that I made a single 671-km dash to the finish, averaging 24 km/h despite the 6000 m of climbing. After my mechanical problem and complete exhaustion of the previous day, I moved from 46th position to cross the finish line in 12th and be one of two over-50-year-olds among the solo racers to break the 65 hours to cover the 1080 km course. This is the magic of ultra-cycling.

Chapter 11

But there are things ultra-cyclists dread more than anything, apart from sleep deprivation to the point where you could close your eyes on your bike and crash. The other greatest challenge comes from the pressure points. Muscles can go through complete energy depletion and cramp and yet recover amazingly quickly. But when pressure points start to hurt, there isn't much that can be done. It's always possible to keep going and just accept the pain, but when the pain comes from one of the three pressure points, you have to carefully evaluate whether the risk of trying to cross the finish line is worth the injury you'll inflict on your body. It usually isn't. Ultra-cycling isn't about crossing a finish line, it's about the experience. The feeling of freedom as you push yourself beyond what you thought you could have done. The communion with the environment. It's pure joy. And even when physical pain is involved, the pleasure usually overcomes all muscle pain. But not so when the pain comes from pressure points.

The pressure points are those parts of your body in constant contact with your bike: your hands, your feet, and your bum.

The constant pressure applied on the feet and hands can leave your extremities with a numb sensation. It's an uncomfortable feeling at first, but not alarming yet. Most ultra-cyclists experience it. Then varying degrees of pain can settle in, sometimes excruciating, sometimes tolerable, and the pain goes away. If the pain dissipates and you can still feel your limbs without any numbness, you're all good. If you don't feel anything anymore, that's when it's becoming serious. And it is counter-intuitive to stop. You've just gone through a great deal of pain, and suddenly, the pain is gone. You push even harder to reach your goal. This can lead to nerve damage. Usually reversible, but not always. Some cyclists have reported having numb hands or feet months after their challenge. Unlike aching muscles, the pain from pressure points isn't something worth fighting. Sometimes your body tells you to stop, and that's the best thing to do. I didn't, and kept riding long distances on it in spite of the pain and numbness; as result, I had to have surgery on my foot to cut out a part of the nerve I had damaged, leaving me not able to walk for four months and not able to cycle for much longer.

Sometimes it's a pain in the butt (pun intended), and the contact with the saddle can yield all kinds of pain, from the most benign to seriously incapacitating ailments. And many things can go wrong with our behinds. A sciatica nerve impingement or numbness of the perineal area can be serious and mandate an immediate stop, rest, stretch, and sometimes anti-inflammatory or other treatments. Luckily, they don't affect experienced cyclists too much, for they can often be avoided with a good bike fit and using a good saddle adapted to your morphology.

The other saddle problems, though, can be more frequent and harder to avoid, particularly for ultra-cyclists as they come from a combination of pressure, friction, and sweat. The longer you ride, the more chance you have of developing them. The most experienced cyclists may be less prone to these than recreational ones, but nobody can escape them. And when they start appearing, the longer you go, the more they become a pain in the buttocks. It can start, though not always, with a simple skin rash from chafing. At this point, it's nothing that a little chamois or baby cream, or even olive oil, couldn't fix. The rash may not go any further. The real problems start with the appearance of a tiny pimple-like protrusion, painful as it usually grows exactly where your full body applies pressure on the saddle. That tiny pimple keeps growing, the more it grows, the greater the pain. It becomes like a cyst, sometimes hard, sometimes filled with pus. The more you ride, the more it continues growing, until any contact with the saddle becomes excruciating.

If you pay attention immediately and treat it with antibiotic cream, change the angle of your saddle (which can lead to other problems) to change your point of contact, and wrap your sensitive area with a special pharmaceutical tape that spreads the pressure over a larger surface, and if you're lucky, it may not become more than an uncomfortable pimple and disappear entirely, even while still riding long daily distances. But most often, the problem keeps increasing at an alarming pace. In a matter of days, it can grow from the size of a raisin to an olive, to a golf ball, and

Chapter 11

even bigger. This is why pro cyclists, who aren't immune from it, call it "the third testicle." Even worse, sometimes you can develop more than one. It's excruciating to a point that it becomes ridiculous to continue. Even pros have pulled out of the Tour de France because of this ailment. Yes, it's a real pain.

To prevent saddle sores, my preference goes to the Bepanthen Pommade (better than the "Bepanthen Crème"). It's a baby cream available in all French and a few other European pharmacies. It's cheaper than cycling creams. If it works for irritated babies when they spend hours in their juice. It also works for ultra-cyclists. It's not bomb-proof to prevent saddle sores, but it's the best I've found. It's more efficient than cycling creams, and I've tested many.

Pierre and Guillaume each have already pushed their limits, gone through all kinds of pain, and prevailed. Their accomplishments so far are not short of heroic. But sometimes even superhuman heroes have to resolve to stop to avoid more serious injuries.

After riding the entire distance from Lourdes to Bagnères without being able to make any contact with the saddle, Guillaume, who otherwise felt incredibly well, came to the wise decision that it wasn't worth risking injuries that would keep him off the bike for months. He described two huge affected areas that threatened to explode at any time.

At 07:20 on day four of the Hautacam Pursuit, it was the end of the adventure for Guillaume. But what an adventure. He had covered 780 km with nearly 18,000 m of elevation in a total time of 70h20' (2 days, 22 hours, and 20 minutes). That's an average of 6000 meters per day, three days in a row, with a bike loaded with luggage, and without any support or assistance. Bravo, Guillaume, for an incredible achievement!

Upon stopping, I asked Guillaume if he was disappointed about not being able to finish.

He said, *"No, I'm not disappointed. It was an amazing adventure, and I pushed myself even more than I ever imagined. I loved it. I learned a lot, and next time I will be ready."*

Guillaume had done his debut in ultra-bikepacking and was already a true champion. A champion who immediately focused his energy on cheering Pierre, the only participant left to ride to the end of the Ultra Bike Pursuit. But the road was still long ahead. Would Pierre succeed?

Pierre on his ninth day continued his epic ride like a metronome. Throughout he had ridden like a well-calibrated machine, stopped to take photos, enjoyed the great scenery, slept longer than all the other participants did, and yet made remarkable daily distances. Pierre never seemed to suffer, even though he certainly did.

Today, he faced a new challenge as France experienced a record high temperature of 36 degrees Celsius, which officials qualified as a heatwave.

As mentioned, September is usually the driest month and the best time of the year to ride an ultra-bikepacking event in the Pyrenees, as these extreme temperatures usually only happen in July or August. The effect of heat and dehydration can seriously hamper the progression of long-distance cyclists, and Pierre, even though he prefers heat to cold, isn't immune to it.

Pierre started early morning from the village of Larrau, where he had finished the toughest climb sets in France the evening before. He first climbed to La Pierre Saint-Martin and described the final section with these words: *"I felt I was riding into another dimension, a world of cliffs and carved stones where you'd expect to meet aliens, but only see roaming sheep and a few other fellow cyclists."*

After taking the time to drink in all the mountain scenery and snap a good set of photos, he zoomed down to climb Ichère and Marie-Blanque. Until then, everything was perfect. Then the grueling midday sun took its toll. It was on the superb but unforgiving slope of Aubisque, after sweating profusely and feeling his face burning, leaving the ski area of Gourette in his wake, that he became exposed to a strong crosswind. The wind is Pierre's kryptonite. He sent me a message:

"I fly like a leaf, blown away wherever the wind blows."

Compounded with the previous hours of suffering in the heat, Pierre really struggled. For the first time since day one, Pierre revealed that he was not a machine. The strength of the wind forced him to a crawl. Every pedal stroke felt heavy. The legendary Aubisque climb, although offering a decent amount of challenge, was nothing compared to all the mountains that Pierre had raced up with ease, yet today, Pierre had found his humanity and moving upwards felt like climbing Everest. When your legs are no longer moving, you're suffering, you're dehydrated, bonking isn't far. Each pedal stroke is a struggle, and the 16-km climb suddenly feels like 160 km. The landscape freezes in time, you're not moving, and you never seem to see the top.

Pierre sent me another message:

"Défaillance énorme dans Aubisque…" (I hit the wall hard in Aubisque.)

Finally, the three giant bike monuments, emblems of the Tour de France, and a herd of friendly horses greeted him at the top. Vultures soared majestically into the wind that had caused Pierre so much trouble. The gentle descent carved into the plunging cliffs of Cirque du Litor was a relief. After Soulor, the descent toward the Argelès valley was enough for Pierre to recover and that's when sent me the full message:

"Défaillance énorme dans Aubisque, mais je suis en train de renaître." (I hit the wall hard in Aubisque, but I'm being reborn.)

The machine may have overheated in the most extreme conditions, but yes, Pierre was still a machine. He made his way up the rolling hills to the Bagnères valley, where I met him as the sun had already disappeared over the mountains and a few clouds started to roll in.

It was too dark to take photos, so I jumped on my bike to join Pierre on his final climb of Aspin. We had a pleasant chat, moving at a good pace, Pierre showing no sign that he had already ridden over 1850 km of non-stop mountain climbs. I left him on top before he plunged and disappeared into the night on his descent to the small village of Arreau, where he found shelter in the booth of a cash machine. There was just enough space for him to take his bike in, and he enjoyed his pizza from a takeout pizza truck before lying down on the hard tile floor, a warm and dry place in case the clouds broke. Too bad he couldn't turn the light off. He could almost have imagined he was sleeping in a hotel room.

Pierre had finished his ninth day, covering 1890 km with over 40,000 m of elevation. He only had 413 km to go to cross the finish line, and it seemed that nothing might be able to stop him. But what loomed ahead were all the most famous and iconic climbs of the Tour de France, including many legendary mountain-stage finishes such as Col du Portet, Luz-Ardiden, and the mighty Hautacam.

Pierre didn't need to cross the finish line, as he'd already made ultra-cycling history. Yet a challenging road remained ahead.

Chapter 12

Alone and Still Going
(September 15)

There aren't many regions in the world that combine as many breathtaking and challenging climbs as the two Pyrenees valleys of Argelès and Saint-Lary. It doesn't get any better. It's a real cycling paradise and a reason why I live at equidistance between these two valleys, which I regularly ride to from home. Between them, the two valleys count no less than 17 major mountain climbs. No other regions feature as many climbs, all starting within a 30-kilometer distance of each other and yet each offering uniquely different and spectacular mountain scenery. Not a single climb vaguely resembles another. The landscape diversity is incredible.

During the Ultimate Pyrenees Ultra Bike Pursuit, Pierre would climb 15 of these, as well as the 28 other climbs spread throughout the Pyrenees mountain chain.

Portet

Today, on day 10, Pierre first climbed Col du Portet. Asphalted for the 2018 Tour de France, its height of 2221 m, a hundred meters higher than Tourmalet with a 0.5% gradient more, boosted it to fame. It instantly dethroned Tourmalet to become the new Tour de France Giant of the Pyrenees. You ride this whole climb in a wide-open valley, with grand, eagle-eye views of the Saint-Lary ski town. If you raise your head toward the top, your eyes meet the switchbacks of Col d'Azet, and farther in the distance those of the Peyragudes ski station and Col de Peyresourde.

In 2019, I had hosted Alex Malone, chief editor of *Cyclist Magazine Australia*, and world-renowned photographer Beardy McBeard (Marcus Enno), for them to write features for the magazine. Malone's headline for the Col de Portet piece was:

"Tougher than Alpe d'Huez, higher than Tourmalet and more stunning than the two combined."

Pierre started with very good legs. *"J'avais des jambes de feu"* (My legs were on fire), he later told me. He pushed and climbed Portet at great speed.

He probably didn't watch the final mountain stage of the 2018 Tour de France. Yumi and I were there, cheering our hero, Chris Froome, as he cracked on the final kilometers, losing all chances to win his fifth Tour de France. Rarely a climb newly featured in the Tour de France has instantly marked history so drastically. It instantly became a climb that would be feared and respected by all cyclists, the ascent that signed the reigning champion's demise. Maybe if Pierre had been supporting Froomey with us two years before, he would have better paced himself, and controlled the fire in his legs. But he didn't, he raced it up.

The lakes

Still filled with energy, Pierre quickly attacked his second set of climbs. Lac de Cap-de-Long and the lakes of Aumar and Aubert are nestled high in the heart of the Néouvielle Natural Reserve and have thus never been featured in the Tour de France. What these climbs lack in international fame, they compensate for by offering world-class cycling, superb and challenging narrow, twisty mountain roads leading to these pristine mountain lakes.

These climbs may even be tougher than those of the mighty Portet or Tourmalet. The narrow roads carved into the cliff feature more switchbacks than you would ever dare count. In *Cyclist Magazine Australia*'s features, Alex Malone described these lakes as one of Europe's cycling gems.

Pierre's speed slowed significantly on the lake climbs. And it was not because he stopped for photos. He suffered the consequences of having pushed too hard on Portet, and struggled throughout his ascent. His legs were no longer on fire. It's mentally challenging when you've prepared yourself to fight your way up a legendary Tour de France climb such as Portet that you swallow easily, and suddenly struggle on a climb that you had never heard about until the organizer of your event set it on your itinerary. A climb that nobody talks about, for it has never seen the fierce battles of the Tour de France. Pierre rides on instinct and feelings. He hadn't planned for this climb to be hard, and when he felt good on the famous Portet he had long wanted to climb, he pushed his heart out. He was a machine, but a little human after all.

During his Ultra Bike adventure, Pierre learned that unknown climbs are often much more challenging than the legendary TDF ones. Luckily, as he struggled his way up, the scenery that unrolled in front of his eyes inspired him. He later said:

"I was really suffering. But the scenery was out of this world. Today was one of the best rides of my life."

Pierre had been saying this daily for the last 10 days. I was delighted to know that the Ultra Bike Pursuit far exceeded all of Pierre's wishes for extreme mountain challenge and sheer beauty[1].

After the technical descent from the lake, he tackled the tough climb of Col d'Azet. A final climb to the now-famous Tour de France's Hourquette d'Ancizan marked the end of his day. After receiving a downpour at the bottom of Hourquette, he reached the top, delighted to find that the sun had returned as he plunged into the descent to Sainte-Marie de Campan, where he checked in a hotel at the base of Tourmalet.

Ultra Bike Pursuit distances are deceiving. Many ultra-cyclists aim to ride between 300 km and 400 km daily on events. Covering these distances

---

1. I invite you to watch a professional videographer's short video of me on the final switchbacks of Lac de Cap-de-Long (velotopo.com).

Chapter 12

in the Pyrenees is an impossible task. Not even a crossing of the Alps could compare to the challenge of the Pyrenees. It had been another big climbing day for Pierre. He covered a distance of only 172 km, during which he climbed a staggering 5000+ m.

In 10 days, Pierre had covered a total of 2073 kilometers with nearly 44,000 meters of elevation gain. His accomplishment was outstanding, but the final stretch was relentless. Tourmalet would take him to the Luz-Argelès valley, Europe's most unique cycling destination featuring the highest concentration of mountain climbs over the shortest distance. The elevation gain remaining was staggering, and many of the greatest climbs of the Tour de France beckoned.

Chapter 13

It Doesn't Get Any Better (September 16)

Tourmalet, the other side

Pierre started his climb of Tourmalet early in the morning with already over 2000 km and much elevation in his legs since he had started the Ultra Bike Pursuit on September 6. The eastern slope of this legendary mountain pass of the Tour de France is dramatically different from the western climb Yvonnick and Chris had finished with. Only a kilometer shorter, the 7.9% average gradient of the 17.4-km climb is similar and it's still a tough climb, but the scenery that unrolls before your eyes with each pedal stroke would have you believe that you're discovering an entirely new mountain in another region of France. It's very typical of the Pyrenees, where the surroundings change every kilometer.

From Sainte-Marie village, you first ride across a forested mountain with streaming waterfalls. A long straight line with a view of Pic du Midi towering just above your head will test your will. The lack of switchback on this constant two-and-half-kilometer 9% grind leading to the ski town of La Mongie makes you feel like you're on a treadmill. When you're climbing a steep road with many close switchbacks, each turn elevates you, and seeing the road you've just cycled below gives you a real sense of progression. Long straight climbs produce the inverse feeling. It's mentally disturbing.

After the steep pitch that crosses La Mongie, the views suddenly open up as you climb the last five kilometers under the ski lift surrounded by soaring peaks. Sheep and cows randomly cross the roads undisturbed. Many people suffer on Tourmalet, but Pierre, who always takes the time to rest well at night, felt great from sunrise. As he continued higher, though, he thought he might be hallucinating when a few dozen llamas, as startled as he was, ran alongside him on the road. Was he going mad?

"I could have been on the Andes of Latin America," he said later.

But the llamas are real, thanks to Eric, the local shepherd who extended his sheep herd with them years ago, and they have now become part of the Tourmalet landscape. Minutes later, they dashed to the side to let him cycle his last kilometer with the giant statue of Octave Lapize reminding him that he was on the most iconic mountain of the Pyrenees.

"Because Tourmalet is such a monument of the Tour de France," he said, *"I only thought it'd be a long tough climb, but it was remarkably beautiful too. It's a stellar climb."*

From the top, he could see the entire valley waking up to the gleaming sun rays, with the road plunging down to the town of Luz-Saint-Sauveur, where he grabbed a snack before heading to the UNESCO World Heritage site of Gavarnie.

Gavarnie & Col des Tentes

The road up to the town of Gavarnie is pleasant, climbing on gentle slopes following the curve of the river with small waterfalls dropping in turquoise pools. Just before reaching the entrance sign of Gavarnie, Pierre was awestruck by the 1000-meter-high natural rock amphitheater that loomed ahead, where Europe's tallest waterfall cascaded 400 meters in a long curtain of water. Nature at its best.

He said: *"Even when you know it's a UNESCO world heritage site, you don't expect such a grand view. It was spectacular."*

Deeply moved by Gavarnie over a hundred years earlier, Victor Hugo described it in his poem "Dieu" ("God") as:

"... a mountain and a wall at the same time; the most mysterious building by the most mysterious architects; it's the colosseum of nature: it's Gavarnie."

Then Pierre climbed Col des Tentes without knowing what to expect. Marmots continually crossed the road in front of his bike. The impressive Pyrenees vultures glided over the mountain ridges. After climbing a road carved into a mountain cliff, the valley suddenly opened up to show a whole series of mountain peaks 3000 meters high, some of them still covered with snow and with vertical walls that made him think he was cycling in Yosemite National Park. On top, he was in awe at the sight and kept saying:

"This and the lake climb yesterday have to be the best climbs I've ridden in my life."

Riding up to Col des Tentes was one of Pierre's highlights, but from the road he could only guess how much more beauty lay behind all these mountains. If he could soar like the vulture circling over his head, he would have discovered an even more magical display of summits, in the middle of which, set at 2800-m high, was the Brèche de Roland (Roland's Breach), an impressive clear-cut through the mountains.

Beyond Col des Tentes

If you remember from "Roland's legend" earlier, over centuries of oral tradition, troubadours transported Roland's heroic Battle of Ronceveau to this Hautes-Pyrénées location. The legend is the same, but now the Saracens army trapped Roland here, at the base of the giant mountains that run between Col des Tentes and Monte Perdido, rather than at Roncevaux Pass.

Unable to escape and certain to die, Roland tried to break Durandal against the cliff. His magical sword cut the 100-meter-deep and 40-meter-wide breach known today as La Brèche de Roland. This mountain clear-cut can be seen from the village of Gèdre, 10 km down the valley. The legend continued in the same manner, with Archangel Michael guiding Roland's thrown sword as it flew over the Pyrenees all the way to Rocamadour.

Chapter 13

Whether you believe the legend or not, Roland's breach is a magnificent site.

An hour's trek from the top of Col des Tentes will have you set your eyes on Roland's Breach. From there, another two hours' walk in the snow will take you up to the Brèche de Roland, where you can stand with one foot in France, the other in Spain, and look at a fabulous mountain panorama on both sides of the border. Maybe once you stand there, you'll start believing in magic.

For experienced trekkers and mountaineers, it's also the start of the climb to Monte Perdido, the highest mountain in the central region and second highest in the Pyrenees. All the mountains surrounding Gavarnie and Col des Tentes hold a special place in my heart for it is where I discovered the magic of mountaineering at age sixteen, climbing the dozens of summits around. Each time I see Gavarnie or climb Col des Tentes, I'm in awe, and it instantly brings back memories about my first mountaineering experience.

On the bike, Col des Tentes is a challenging ascent on its own, and Pierre had just climbed Tourmalet before, but his day wasn't over yet. He still had to climb to the Cirque du Troumouse. He would then decide there, depending on his legs, if he would attempt to finish the entire course in a day or take an extra day. If his legs were good, he wanted to cross the finish line today, but he still had three tough mountains to go. And if the names Luz-Ardiden and Hautacam spoke for themselves to anybody watching the Tour de France, he had no idea about Troumouse.

He had barely descended three kilometers from Col des Tentes when his rear tire blew up, his first flat of the adventure. But it wasn't a simple flat. He had purchased this new endurance tire in a small bike shop three days earlier. Because Pierre rides so much, he prefers the heavy-duty marathon tires to the light, high-rolling efficiency racing tires, a choice he makes for two reasons: to get better mileage out of his tires, and to avoid flats. That new tire was defective. The metal bedding was completely rusted, the sewing of the material around it was coming apart. The tire may have never been used, but it was clear that it had been stored many years in a humid environment and the rusty metal edges had eaten into the fabric. Even with a new tube, the tire threatened to explode from all its edges. It was unsafe to try riding on it.

To follow the event's rules, Pierre hitched a ride to purchase a new tire in Luz and returned to the same place he had had the puncture, wasting nearly three hours. It was mid-afternoon by then. This mechanical incident had destroyed his chance of crossing the finish line on this same day; however, his spirit was undaunted.

Troumouse

Amid thrilling settings and having lost three hours, an invigorated Pierre raced up the first third of Troumouse. Then it became really difficult for him, as he had pushed too hard at the base of the climb. The climb was three times the length and much tougher than he expected. But the harder it got, the more magnificent the scenery became.

He said: *"I kept thinking, this is the most beautiful place. Then as I thought it couldn't be any better, and I'd reached what looked to be the top, it wasn't, it was a plateau that was even more spectacular. But that wasn't the top. The road kept going up."*

Troumouse was another climb where I had guided the *Cyclist Magazine Australia* team. They published a 16-page main feature about it and chief editor Alex Malone told me, *"This has got to be one of the absolute best."* He wrote:

"Beyond the barriers of the pro peloton, Cyclist Magazine heads to the Hautes-Pyrénées to discover roads free from the pressure of the sport's biggest races. Equally stunning as their more famous neighbors, the Cirque de Troumouse and Col des Tentes should be part of every cyclist's bucket list."

Reaching the third and final plateau, in the middle of this natural amphitheater that is the Cirque du Troumouse, was what Pierre described as his apotheosis.

He said: *"It wasn't only the most amazing climb in my life. It was more stunning than any stuff you could dream about. It was even better than the other climbs. I didn't think that'd be possible. I was in awe."*

Pierre took his time on the technical descent, featuring over 50 switchbacks that lead back to the road in the valley.

Luz-Ardiden

The next ascent was none other than Luz-Ardiden, the legendary mountain finish of the Tour de France. This was the famous climb where Lance Armstrong caught his handlebars on the musette of a spectator, resulting in him crashing onto the asphalt before racing up in what would become one of the most epic historical battles. Yumi and I were there to witness his domination of Jan Ullrich. There are mountain climbs grander than life, and Luz-Ardiden is one of them.

The road had just been resurfaced and was buttery smooth and fast. The switchbacks offered perfect curves that made them a pleasure both to ascend and to descend. Pierre arrived on top in the late evening and felt great.

He told me, *"I'll stop by the town below, and if I can still find food, I'll continue to the finish."*

He was still a long way from the finish, but Pierre was lucky to arrive minutes before the supermarket closed its doors. Having stocked up on food and drinks, he raced his way down the valley to reach the base of the mighty Hautacam as the setting sun dropped out of sight, leaving a dim light that only showed the contours of the mountain silhouetted against the sky.

Final mountain climb

How tough could this last mountain climb be? After all, it was less than 16 kilometers, a good two kilometers shorter than Tourmalet that he had climbed with ease in the morning. Hautacam has been a mountain finish climb of the Tour de France on various occasions. Each time it was a decisive climb for the pro racers. It's the Alpe-d'Huez of the Pyrenees but more scenic, and tougher too.

During the day, the landscape never stops changing, but at night all Pierre could experience was the irregularity of the slope. When his light flashed onto a sign that read a 9.5% average gradient over the next kilometer, and when that kilometer started with a descent, he knew the climb coming would be grueling. A strong cyclist with fresh legs doesn't mind a few 15% pitches. But by this time, Pierre had already ridden 2200 km with over 50,000 meters of climbing since the start of the event. And on that same day, he had already climbed Tourmalet, Col des Tentes, Cirque du Troumouse, and Luz-Ardiden, all very challenging ascents. To make matters worse, the last kilometers were exposed to strong head- and crosswinds that hindered his progress even more.

Pierre, after all he climbed today, after his weeks of intense riding, and with a loaded bike, reached the top of Tramassel in an astonishing 1h36'. An unbelievable achievement.

After donning a jacket, he descended carefully, making sure he stayed alert. The worst thing would be a few seconds of inattention. By this point, muscles still respond, but the general fatigue ultra-athletes feel cannot be properly described. It's not exhaustion. The body has already gone through various states of exhaustion. Only the mind keeps pushing the body forward, all pains have gone. But the body is in such a deep state of fatigue, it doesn't know it anymore. With the finish within grasp, you are filled with endorphins and adrenaline, you almost don't feel any pain or fatigue. But that's your brain lying to you, consciously or unconsciously. Your body only needs a fraction of a second of inattention from your brain to collapse. When you're tired, mistakes can quickly happen. Especially when the finish looms not too far ahead: you can't let your guard down. It's not over until you pass the finish line and stop.

The last stretch took him on rural roads over rolling hills. Pierre reached the finish line in Bagnères de Bigorre just before one in the morning, after an impressive final day during which he rode 265 km with a staggering 7300 m of elevation gain. A monster of a day to end an epic mountain ride.

He'd done it. He'd achieved the impossible.

When I designed this grueling course over spectacular mountain roads, I wasn't convinced I'd be able to finish it, and didn't know if anybody would even attempt it. This is why I designed shorter courses with a range of itineraries starting from 550 km.

The 2300-km course, the Ultimate Pyrenees Pursuit, includes a staggering 55,700 m of elevation gain. It's the length of the Tour de France with three times more elevation that ultra-cyclists ride while carrying their gear, without drafting inside a peloton and without any support.

Pierre Charles, the first ultra-cyclist to cross the finish of the Ultimate Pyrenees Pursuit, accomplished this feat in 10 days, 16 hours, and 45 minutes (256h45').

This is a daily average of 5200 m of elevation over a distance of 215 km. The full route includes 43 major climbs and Arnostéguy, the toughest climb in France. Arnostéguy is the French version of Angliru and Zoncolan, both considered the world's toughest climbs, except that combined with the ascent of Col d'Arthé, it's more difficult and the descents are far more technical.

The Ultra Bike Pursuit isn't the Everest of ultra bikepacking, it's the K2 of the sport! Everest is the mountain people flock to, hoping to add the prestigious name to their record of achievements. K2 is the mountain for the strongest in a quest to explore their limits, experience the highest degree of freedom, and attain enlightenment.

On September 17, 2020, before 01:00, Pierre Charles made history. He became a bikepacking legend.

This could be a record, but Pierre, like many other ultra-bikepacker, isn't interested in records; he just wants to explore his limits and enjoy the most amazing roads and climbs. That's what he did.

After the finish line, and sleeping a few hours, later in the morning he sent me this message:

"Thank you so much! I return home with my eyes filled with stars. These were the most amazing moments of my life as a cyclist! Forever etched in my memory 😊😊😊."

Just as his cycling odyssey did not even start with the Ultra Bike Pursuit, nor did it end on the finish line. Not only had Pierre ridden his bike thousands of kilometers to the start of the Ultra Bike Pursuit, the next day he would return home, as always, riding his bike across France. At least his holiday was coming to an end. He could finally rest at work, on his laden messenger bike, hauling equipment and making deliveries all day long.

I wouldn't be surprised if, in the close future, Pierre will be headlining cycling and endurance sports and adventure magazines, maybe even appearing on TV. He's only 28 years old and still has millions of kilometers of roads to ride and hundreds of mountains to climb.

Pierre may have stolen the show, but he wasn't the only ultra-cyclist to accomplish a phenomenal achievement on the Ultra Bike Pursuit. Yvonnick, Chris, Alex, and Guillaume's were also remarkable.

Results

Here is a summary of their accomplishments (daily averages are calculated per 24 hours with a rule of three. The result is the equivalence for a 24-hour period of the total elevation or distance done within the finishing time).

Ultimate Pyrenees Pursuit: 2300 km / 55,700 m
Pierre Charles
10 days, 16 hours, and 45 minutes (256h45')
Daily Average: 215 km / 5200 m

Tourmalet Hardcore Pursuit: 1100 km / 22,000 m
Yvonnick Brossier
4 days, 2 hours, and 35 minutes (98h35')
Daily Average: 267 km / 5340 m

Chris Jackson
4 days, 15 hours, and 11 minutes (111h11')
Daily Average: 234 km / 4750 m

Hautacam Hardcore Pursuit: 1200 km / 33,000 m
Guillaume Labedan
Stopped due to saddle problems after covering 780 km / 18,000 m in 2 days, 22 hours, and 20 minutes (70h20')
Daily Average: 266 km / 6145 m

Hautacam Discovery Pursuit: 550 km / 12,400 m
Alex Montegut
1 day, 15 hours, and 54 minutes (39h54')
Daily Average: 330 km / 7460 m

It Doesn't Get Any Better

Chapter 13

It Doesn't Get Any Better

Chapter 13

Conclusion

In Pursuit of Life-Changing Challenges

I put all my passion and knowledge into designing the Ultra Bike Pursuit, and I am pleased that the itinerary truly offers the best of these mountains and regions.

The reward came when a well-traveled cyclist like Pierre said:

"These were the most amazing moments of my life as a cyclist! Forever etched in my memory."

Or local Pyrenean Yvonnick said:

"The routes you designed were tough but superb. I didn't think I would have to face so many mountains: it never stopped. Really, thank you! You took us through places with sublime landscapes, which even being from the Pyrenees, I would probably never have known by bike without your event. It's a new practice of cycling, and without a doubt, the best experience I have had in this sport. Thanks to you for making me discover this."

Or local first-timers like Alex and Guillaume said:

"A fantastic first experience for me with superb organization."

"Wonderful discovery of ultra bikepacking!"

Or experienced British bikepacker Chris described it as:

"The full Ultra Pursuit course is a staggeringly challenging ride to complete. World's toughest? Well, I doubt there'd ever be a consensus agreement on what that is, but it has to be up there amongst them. One of the most beautiful? Well, that is unquestionably correct."

This tells me I succeeded. I was true to myself. I shared my passion for the sport and the love I have for my Pyrenees mountains. And I hope that more cyclists will come to experience all of the Pyrenees' beauty and challenge, and to explore their limits.

Why do people explore their limits?

There are many reasons. Each participant had their own, and you can read some of their ride reports on the Ultra Bike Pursuit website. And you may also have your reasons.

I can only describe mine.

Since childhood, I was a dreamer. I dreamed of following in the footsteps of Jacques Cousteau. I dreamed of traveling to remote destinations. I dreamed of wild mountains, dense jungles, and tropical oceans. But both my family and French society suffocated me, repeatedly tried to kill my dreams, always reminding me that world explorer was not a profession.

I also dreamed of sports, another thing my family would not support. They believed it wasn't for me, that athlete wasn't a job either.

I could have given up and lived the life others wanted me to live. But I didn't. I fought against all odds to live the life I always wanted. Because I didn't want to live someone's else life. I wanted it to be my life.

When I set out on the three-year Central American Sea Kayak Expedition, to paddle 5000 kilometers of wild oceans and up rivers through malaria-infested jungles with the goals of experiencing and documenting the lifestyle of indigenous people, I accomplished a dream. My expedition partner and I achieved the longest, maybe toughest sea kayak expedition ever recorded.

We faced storms at sea, sharks, crocodiles, armed bandits, millions of biting bugs, tropical diseases, and our own mortality. I didn't expect to succeed on this expedition. I didn't plan to die either, but I knew there was a high possibility this would happen. It was a risk I was willing to take, just to feel alive.

Life isn't what society or your parents decided for you. It's not listening to your boss every day. It's what you make out of it. Most people never accomplish their dream. I didn't want to live an empty, meaningless life.

Cousteau, Hemingway, London, Saint-Exupery, and many other explorers inspired my childhood and my entire life. I preferred to live a short life that was mine than a long dull life that wasn't.

Of course, I was scared. Even terrified at times. I almost quit on more than one occasion. But I didn't.

It is when I explore my limits that I feel most alive. It is when I go beyond what I even thought possible that I better understand who I am as a human being. It doesn't have to be in an ultra-endurance sport. When I first set foot on the wild jungle island of Siberut in Indonesia, I knew I had to return to explore that jungle and live with its fascinating indigenous hunter-gatherers. I left everything behind. I risked it all. I gave up all the comfort and security of everything I knew. It was almost naked and entirely vulnerable that I immersed myself into a world and culture I knew nothing about. It was not a sport. It was living a simple life amongst one of the most traditional and fascinating indigenous tribes on the planet, in one of the harshest environments. I had to explore my limits to do so. It was a revelation. One of the most inspiring experiences in my life[1].

There are many reasons to push your physical and mental limits. Ultra-endurance sports may be the fastest way to do so. You don't need to venture on a three-year sea kayak expedition across Central America. You don't need to live four months deep in the jungle with a group of hunter-gathers. You don't need to fight your entire childhood and through adulthood to become who you want to be when all your surroundings try to prevent you from being that person.

With ultra-endurance sports, in a few days you find your true self. Two days is all it may take.

It's difficult to describe how many emotions we experience during an event like this one. From the lowest moments and deepest levels of pain to the ecstatic, euphoric highs, it's almost like squeezing a full year of adventure and human encounters into a few days' timeframe.

In the space of a few hours, you can go through sensations and emotions others may never experience in their lifetime. There is no more work

---

1. View photos and read more about the Mentawai (www.jpsoule.com).

pressure, stress from the petty things of life. You are free, vulnerable, and alone with yourself. There is no more lying to yourself. It's only you, the real you, living your life, facing your own challenge, facing yourself.

There is no competition with others. It's all about being in tune with yourself. In the space of a few hours or days, all your physical pains will transform into the most amazing feelings. Sometimes, it feels like a deep state of meditation. Sometimes you may have hallucinations or wander into different worlds. Sometimes you may suddenly focus and see the solutions to all the problems you couldn't resolve. All the ideas you couldn't express clearly suddenly appear as the clearest, most logical concepts. I often get new ideas, and sometimes even a full chapter for one of my books flows through me when I'm on a long-distance challenge.

When you reach your physical limits. When your body begs you to quit, and your mind takes over, you go beyond your limits. It's more than a revelation. It's enlightenment.

Everything thereafter becomes easy. You'll never think the same way. Impossible is no longer part of your vocabulary. Everything is possible, it's all in the head.

It's all in YOUR head. And the more you push your limits, the stronger your head becomes. The more irrelevant the word *impossible* becomes. The more you are able to achieve all your goals and live all your dreams. The more you can be yourself, and not someone else defined by decades of artificial formatting.

I love exploring my limits just to be myself and feel free. It's a pleasure that goes far beyond any pain you'll ever experience in ultra-endurance. It's what feeling alive is.

Are you living the life you've always wanted to? Or are you living someone else's life?

Do you really know who you are and what you are capable of?

What are your dreams? Have you realized or even attempted to realize them?

The Ultra Bike Pursuit, or any ultra-endurance challenge, may be the best doorway to your own life's pursuit and to answer all your questions.

Don't hesitate. Hesitation is the difference between the doers, finishers and winners and the others. All you need is Two Wheels and Will for the world to be yours. Just try it!

If you've enjoyed *Two Wheels and a Will*, your honest review can help me continue to write new books. I can't express how grateful I would be if you followed this link to leave a review:

https://mybook.to/amazon-2wheelsreview

Thank you,

Colin Hunter (Jean-Philippe)

Addendum

Racing across Europe

After a complicated winter, in the early months of 2019 I was in the worst shape I had ever been, except for a couple of years when I suffered from recurring malaria 25 years ago. When you're 53 years old, it's demoralizing to gain weight and lose your fitness by the day as soon as you stop training. My morale spiraled down as quickly as my form.

My wife, Yumi, an accomplished mountain endurance road cyclist, had placed first and fourth woman respectively in the Luchon-Bayonne and Tour du Mont-Blanc mountain races. Tour du Mont-Blanc was the holy grail of one-day mountain road cycling events. She wanted something tougher to test her limits, but it seemed nothing could challenge her more than that event.

In March 2019, she searched the internet for her ultimate summer challenge. One day she told me she had found a 7400-kilometer non-stop race across Europe from Norway to Spain that crossed the Alps and 15 countries. Less than a dozen solo cyclists had crossed the finish line the previous year, and no pair succeeded. She wanted us to enter as a pair and set the record. We would be the first.

When she told me that, I laughed and entirely dismissed the idea. First, we couldn't attempt it, as we already had a couple of cycling tours booked during that period. The business commitments were a great excuse for me to bail out. My wife was in excellent form, she had kept riding throughout the winter, while I completely stopped to finish writing and publish my adventure travel memoir *Dancing with Death*. I had spent nearly 18 hours a day staring at a computer screen for six full months.

I was 86 kg, nine kilograms over my fitness weight. Nine kilograms I had gained in less than six months. I had almost not touched the bike in four months. I had just started cycling again and struggled to ride 100 kilometers on a fairly flat road, and she wanted us to race the world's longest and maybe toughest cycling event as a pair in less than three months. I didn't even look like a cyclist. I looked more like Santa Claus – maybe with a red outfit and a few reindeer, I would not have looked out of place in Norway. But there was no way I'd embarrass myself by taking on a race from North Cape to ride non-stop on sleepless days for relentless weeks all the way to Tarifa in Spain, when I couldn't even ride a single long day.

In March 2019, I was simply unable to ride even an easy day in the mountains. Three months of training would never be enough time to gain half the fitness I would need to put myself on the start line. I wouldn't have the slimmest chance of ever finishing such a challenge.

The night she told me of her plan for us, though I turned it down, I couldn't close my eyes. I got out of bed and spent the whole night on the internet looking for information, checking the routes, and reading blogs. There wasn't much about it, but I found other, similar races, and I binge-watched every video clip and read all the interviews about every similar event. It mesmerized me. I didn't know these types of races existed. It was crazy. What kind of people would be mad enough to do this type of thing?

Yumi understood my reply. It was logical. We had work and a commitment to our customers. She also knew that even if in my youth I had managed to get in shape after months of traveling without training, those years were behind me and there was just not enough time. I would never be able to do it. She continued surfing the internet to look for her own challenge for that year. But I couldn't stop thinking about it. It was haunting me day and night.

After three sleepless nights, I thought: *We only live once. And we have to live our lives to the fullest. If we don't, what's the point of even living? We can't let all the things that burden our lives guide us.*

At the same time, one of our two groups in that period wanted to change to later dates. If only we could move the other group a few days, we could make it work. I contacted our clients, who were happy to move their dates. It was perfect; we were able to clear our schedule to fly to Norway. I didn't tell Yumi until I was purchasing the tickets on the internet. She was taken aback, bewildered yet pleasantly surprised. Thus, planning and training began.

This is how, at the age of 53, I discovered the sport of ultra-bikepacking, and what an experience it was. It was a revelation. This attempt at racing across Europe as a pair will be the subject of my next cycling book.

Visit www.jpsoule.com and join my reading group to be notified of its release.

More Books by the Author

Your free eBook!

Sign up for alerts about new releases and a free download of *Dining with My Cannibal Friend*.

Dining with My Cannibal Friend

"You are big and white. You have a lot of meat and you look delicious!"

Six thousand words are all it takes for you to join the award-winning author of *Dancing with Death* on a grand travel adventure.

In this short but gripping narration, he will guide you through a world few could imagine—where the inhabitants practice ritual cannibalization. True stories are often better than fiction.

Your free eBook:
https://getbook.at/cannibal

More Books by the Author

You'll love Jean-Philippe's epic memoirs. Whether you like extreme endurance sports, the wild outdoors, survival stories, thrilling adventures, or inspiring memoirs, you'll be blessed with real-life stories that will leave you in awe.

Many readers mentioned that once they started reading *I, Tarzan* or *Dancing with Death*, it was impossible for them to put these books down. These page-turners read like novels, but the stories are all too real and will leave you on the edge of your seat. If you've ever wondered what it's like to be an adventurer, reading these will have you experience it in ways that go beyond the imaginable.

More Books by the Author

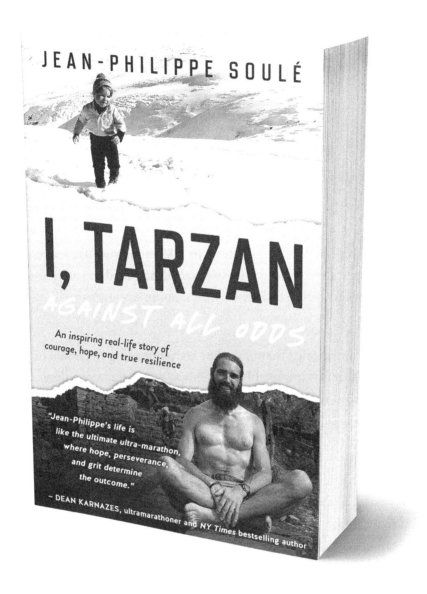

"Any reader who believes that early adversity sets a life's course in stone should read I, Tarzan: Against All Odds."
— D. Donovan, Senior Reviewer, Midwest Book Reviews

More Books by the Author

I, Tarzan: Against All Odds

From the award-winning author of *Dancing with Death* comes an epic memoir that will delight fans of *The Glass Castle*, *Wild*, and *Unbroken*, as well as *Educated* and *Can't Hurt Me*. The gripping *I, Tarzan* is a deep journey into the author's innermost secrets that will have you questioning your own self-understanding and life goals.

From the back cover:

> By age thirteen, I was an alcoholic—anything to numb myself from my world of emotional abuse.
> That wasn't who I wanted to be.
> My dreams of adventure and exploration were so far out of reach. I'd never become Tarzan. I'd never become Jacques Cousteau.
> But I was wrong.
> This is my story . . .

Celebrity endorsements for *I, Tarzan*:

> *"Jean-Philippe's life is like the ultimate ultra-marathon, where hope, perseverance, and grit determine the outcome.* I, Tarzan: Against All Odds *is his story of redemption and remembrance that inspires and energizes the reader to believe that far-reaching dreams can come true. Jean-Philippe proves that your attitude determines your altitude — and high he climbs in this must-read memoir!"*
> — Dean Karnazes, ultramarathoner and *NY Times* bestselling author

> *"Marco Polo meets Tom Sawyer,* I, Tarzan *is the roller-coaster chronicle of Jean-Philippe Soule's early life of challenge and adventure. . . . This is a story of success, wrought in the fires of despair and wrapped up in good old-fashioned storytelling."*

— Ian Adamson, author and world's most celebrated adventure racer

"*I, Tarzan* tears at the heartstrings and brings to remembrance every unfulfilled childhood dream. Jean-Philippe's story lends us the courage to see them as future possibilities. His grit and determination inspire and electrify. An emotional journey of enduring accomplishment. I highly recommend it."

— C. J. Anaya, *USA Today* bestselling and multi-award-winning author of *The Healer* series

Read *I, Tarzan: Against All Odds*:
https://mybook.to/tarzan2

Jean-Philippe is currently working on new books.
Find out more about the author and all his books and view his award-winning photos at www.jpsoule.com.

Dancing with Death
An Inspiring Real-Life Story of Epic Travel Adventure

Fans of Jon Krakauer will devour this gripping tale of adventure, survival, and a search for life's deeper meaning.

The winner of four international book awards and an Amazon bestseller, *Dancing with Death: An Epic and Inspiring Real-Life Travel Adventure* depicts an enlightening and oftentimes grueling journey as the compelling narrative recounts the author's three-year sea kayaking adventure, covering 3,000 miles through seven countries following the flow of the Atlantic and Pacific coastlines through Central America.

How many of us fantasize of walking away from the daily grind of the American Dream to embark on a grand adventure? That's exactly what former French Special Forces Commando Jean-Philippe Soulé did in real life — abandoning his cushy Microsoft job to launch into a three-year kayaking adventure of unforgettable discovery and life-threatening danger in Central America.

In 1998, Jean-Philippe and his travel partner Luke Shullenberger shed the trappings of comfortable civility to venture into the Central American Sea Kayak Expedition 2000 — an ambitious quest to paddle all the way from California to Panama. The bold expedition would take the two men across 3,000 miles of the remote and wild Central American coastline, spanning three years, seven countries, and countless once-in-a-lifetime experiences.

Now, twenty years later, Jean-Philippe Soulé reflects on this incredible and enlightening journey in *Dancing with Death* — a compelling real-life

More Books by the Author

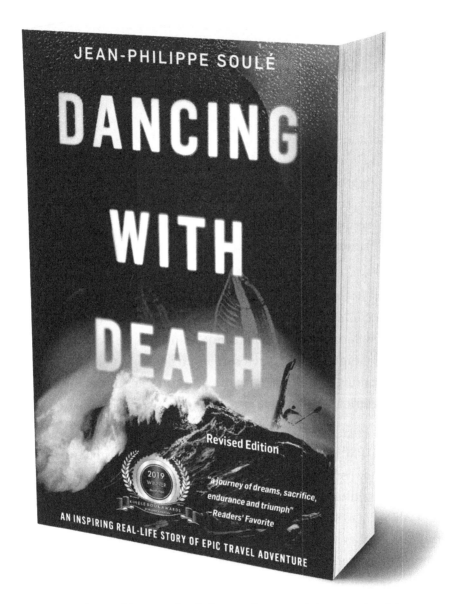

"An unforgettable escapade of ultimate danger and discovery, inspiring less intrepid souls . . ."
— Joel R. Dennstedt, author of Guanjo

travel memoir that documents the tales of exploration, endurance, and self-discovery that Soulé and Shullenberger experienced as they kayaked across the world's most exquisite and treacherous waters. Readers of all ages will be inspired as they follow Jean-Philippe and Luke on this extraordinary transformational voyage — testing their limits, exploring new cultures, and learning that life is what we make it, if only we dare to reach for our dreams.

A FEW EDITORIAL REVIEWS:

"Thrilling adventure, soulful insights and crisp, fast-paced writing."
— IndieReader

"What the power of human will can accomplish is inspiring, emotional, and empowering."
— The Book Review Directory

"A fast-paced story that will grip you and inspire you. Highly recommended."
— The Wishing Shelf

FROM THE AUTHOR:

Dancing with Death will take you on the ride of a lifetime. It's a rollercoaster of resilience, rare encounters, and moments that will leave you on the edge of your seat, as well as a fascinating account of adventure, passion, and an insight into our very own lives. I hope reading this book will inspire you to pursue your passions and dreams.
— Jean-Philippe Soulé.

Read *Dancing with Death*:
https://mybook.to/dwd2

About the Author

Find out more about the author and all his books and view his award-winning photos at www.jpsoule.com. You can connect with him on: Goodreads, Facebook and Amazon.

Information about bikepacking events: ww.ultrabikepursuit.com

Information about custom cycling tours: www.velotopo.com

About the Author

Jean-Philippe Soulé is the award-winning and bestselling author of real-life adventure and travel memoirs published under his full name. He also writes in different genres, using pen names to differentiate among them. Colin Hunter is his pseudonym for cycling books.

He served as a French Special Forces mountain commando; led jungle, mountain, and kayaking expeditions; and traveled all over the world to produce photo documentaries.

He started cross-country skiing and cycling races while living in Japan. In 1996, he won the prologue of the UCI Asia Tour de Hokkaido, despite having no prior experience in road racing. Jean-Philippe credits his win to a strong cardio capacity after having recently swapped mountaineering and cross-country skiing for cycling. He raced track for a few years in the United States. He is also a certified USA Cycling Coach and licensed professional French cycling guide. He offers 20 years of experience in designing and guiding unique cycling tours to Europe's best mountain destinations, and he has organized multiple cycling fundraising events.

In 2019, he and his wife, Yumi, set the record as the first pair to finish the 7,400+ km ultra-cycling race from Norway to Spain. In 2020, he raced the 1080 km ultra-bikepacking championship stage in the Sultana of Oman.

Bikepacking combines his passion for ultra-cycling, travel, and adventure. He is the organizer of the Ultra Bike Pursuit bikepacking events that cover the entire mountain chain of his native Pyrenees.

Through his books, Jean-Philippe shares his passion for life. He inspires others to believe in their dreams, find their true self, and live the life they've always desired. He believes that nothing is impossible. We can all do what we set our mind to, we just need to believe in ourselves and go for it.

Made in the USA
Middletown, DE
03 November 2023

41925592R00116